ALL THE COMMANDMENTS OF GOD

–Volume II

Hidden Treasures from the Books of Galatians,
Ephesians, Philippians & Colossians

Unlocking the Mystery to Inheriting
All the Blessings of God

DR. ESTHER V. SHEKHER

WESTBOW
PRESS®
A DIVISION OF THOMAS NELSON
& ZONDERVAN

WestBow Press books may be ordered through booksellers or by contacting:

WestBow Press
A Division of Thomas Nelson & Zondervan
1663 Liberty Drive
Bloomington, IN 47403
www.westbowpress.com
1 (866) 928-1240

Scripture taken from the New King James Version®. Copyright © 1982 by Thomas Nelson. Used by permission. All rights reserved.

Scripture quotations noted KJV are taken from the Holy Bible, King James Version.

THE HOLY BIBLE, NEW INTERNATIONAL VERSION®, NIV® Copyright © 1973, 1978, 1984, 2011 by Biblica, Inc.® Used by permission. All rights reserved worldwide.

Our Contact Address:
Christ Rules
Phone: Dr. Esther: +1-626-450-5973
Michelle: +1-480-251-1979
Darla: +1-209-401-1696
Email: christrulesnations@gmail.com;
christrulesus@hotmail.com
Website: www.christrulesnations.org /
www.allthecommandmentsofgod.com
Facebook: ChristRulesNations

ISBN: 978-1-9736-4994-6 (sc)
ISBN: 978-1-5127-3334-1 (e)

WestBow Press rev. date: 06/17/2019

Print information available on the last page.

The Great Commission Of Christ

"Go and make disciples
of all the nations,

baptizing them in the name
of the Father and the Son
and the Holy Spirit.

Teach these new disciples to obey all the
commands I have given you."
(Matt.28:19-20/NLT)

This Book is dedicated
To my Beloved Savior and Lord Jesus Christ
Who has given me the Free Gift of Eternal Life.
And Christ Rules My Heart.

Christ Must Rule Our Hearts
Christ Must Rule Our Lives
Christ Must Rule Our Cities
Christ Must Rule Our Nations
For Christ Rules Our Universe.

Contents

Part I Book Of Galatians

Part IV Book Of Colossians

Foreword

As a long time television producer and host, I am required to consider hundreds of books each year for my daily Homekeepers program. No one has ever made the profound impact on my own life like Dr. Esther V. Shekher and her books, ALL THE COMMANDMENTS OF GOD, Volumes 1 and 2. The first time I looked through them, I realized that she has highlighted an important "truth", sorely needed in the church today.

Volume 2 dissects the writings of the Apostle Paul spotlighting the blessings of obedience along with the consequences of disobedience. These books, uniquely formatted, are a refreshing rain in a desert of writings about earthly prosperity and "self" fulfillment. They offer a valuable Biblical resource whether used for personal benefit, a group setting or pulpit series.

Arthelene Rippy
CHRISTIAN TELEVISION NETWORK

Author's Heart

Introduction

I give all praise, glory and honor to our Sovereign God, who, by His grace, has enabled me to finish this second book in the series entitled "All the Commandments of God," which was birthed into my spirit by the Lord God Almighty.

It is my desire that I place this unique book, which reveals the **hidden treasures of God's Word,** into every one of your hands, to enrich your lives. Against all odds, the Holy Spirit of God has enabled me to highlight all the Commandments of God from the Epistles of Apostle Paul in this divinely directed book.

The commandments are the desires of God's heart; His instructions for us to live a pleasing life before Him. Whenever an instruction of the Lord is followed by rewards or consequences and sometimes both, it is a command. Sometimes they are just direct commandments from the Lord without any rewards or consequences following and we must obey them just because the Lord said so. There is nothing more important than obeying the commandments of God.

Purpose of the Book

Scripture says, if we diligently obey the voice of the Lord our God, to *observe carefully all His commandments, then the blessings will come upon us* and overtake us. Hence I sought the Lord inquiring, "What are the commandments that we ought to obey to inherit all Your blessings?" After praying much in the Spirit for the past ten years, I received this awesome revelation from the Lord. (Deut.28:1)

The first book in the series from the Gospels of Matthew and John covers almost all the major topics in Christian faith. I have written this second book for those who long for a *much deeper walk with the Lord*. In this book, I have brought out the commandments, the precious truths of God's Word, His hidden treasures, in the simplest format from the Epistles of Paul to the Galatians, Ephesians, Philippians and Colossians, which are applicable to us even today.

For *all Scripture is given by inspiration of God*, and is profitable for doctrine, for reproof, for correction, for instruction in righteousness. (2 Tim.3:16)

Conclusion

Apostle Paul states, *"Join together in following my example*, brothers and sisters."* (Phil.3:17)

And, *"Be ye followers of me*, even as I also am of Christ." (1 Cor.11:1/KJV)

Since Apostle Paul himself exhorts us, saying, **"Put it into practice—whatever you have learned, or received or heard from me, or seen in me,"** some of the commandments, which are exemplary, are taken from Apostle Paul's life and experiences on earth; for the rewards and consequences following the commandments are very clear. When we obey these commandments, we will also receive the blessings, as stated by Apostle Paul. (Phil. 4:9/NIV)

I am confident that this book will bless you beyond your comprehension, just as it has blessed and enriched me writing it for you.

Acknowledgements

Special thanks to my loving family members for their help, encouragement and support in the ministry. I thank my dear friend, Monica, who helped me compile this book. I am also indebted to all those who stood with me in prayer for the release of this book.

PS: The Asterisk symbol (*) used in the book indicates Author's life experiences.

The text under each commandment table, indicated with a bullet, denotes the Author's commentary which will help the reader better understand the commandments of God.

Galatia – Modern Day Turkey

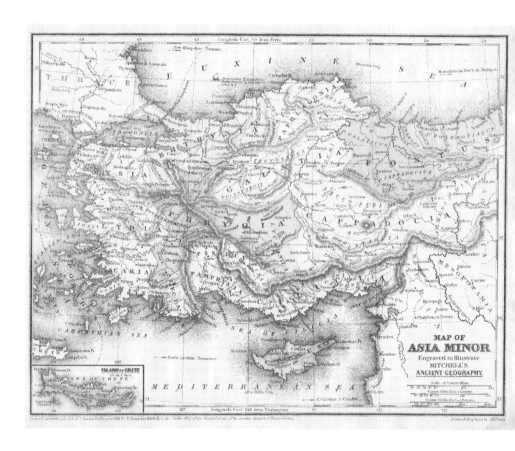

Book Of Galatians

Apostle Paul wrote this epistle to the **Churches of Galatia** in the year A.D. 49. Paul and Barnabas together evangelized and established these churches in the cities of Pisidian Antioch, Iconium, Lystra and Derbe, during their *first missionary journey.* (Gal.1:1-2; Acts 13,14; 22:3)

Paul was a man thoroughly trained in the Law, under a great scholar named Gamaliel. (Acts 22:3)

The main theme of this letter is that we receive Salvation by grace through *faith in Jesus Christ* and not by the works of the law.

*Purpose...*Apostle Paul explains that ceremonial laws, such as, circumcision, under the old covenant, have nothing to do with Salvation under the new covenant, which is only by God's grace in Christ.

In this epistle, Paul also emphasizes that we, the NT believers, receive the *power of the Holy Spirit* to live a victorious life, only by faith in the Lord Jesus Christ and not by the works of the law. (Gal.3:2-5)

Special features... This letter contains a list of the "Fruit of the Holy Spirit" and also a detailed catalogue of the "Works of the Flesh." (Gal.5:19-23)

Paul clarifies that the true gospel of Christ involves freedom from sin and also freedom from the ceremonial, sacrificial and civil laws of the Old Testament.

Freedom in Christ involves living by the power of the Holy Spirit and fulfilling the law of Christ.

"Put it into practice - whatever you have learned, or received or heard from me, or seen in me," says Apostle Paul. (Phil. 4:9/NIV; 2 Tim.3:16)

1. Believe In Jesus & Inherit The Blessings of Abraham

COMMANDMENTS OF GOD FOR US TO OBEY	REWARDS FOR OBEDIENCE/ SUPPORTING SCRIPTURES
1. Be those who are of faith in Jesus Christ. (Gal.3:7,9,14) 2. Believe God just as Abraham did. (Gal.3:6)	1. For it will be accounted to you for *righteousness*. (Gal.3:6; Rom.4:24) 2. Only those who believe in Jesus Christ are *children of Abraham*. (Gal.3:1,7/NIV) 3. Those who are of faith are *blessed* along with Abraham, the man of faith. (Gal.3:9/NIV) 4. God would *justify the nations* by faith. (Gal.3:8) 5. That you might receive the *promise of the Spirit* through faith in Jesus Christ. (Gal.3:14, 22) 6. You will receive the *inheritance in Christ* which God gave to Abraham by promise. (Gal.3:18) 7. That you might be *justified by faith* in Christ. (Gal.3:24) 8. You are *all sons of God* through faith in Christ Jesus. (Gal.3:26) 9. If you belong to Christ, then you are *Abraham's seed, and heirs* according to the promise. (Gal.3:29/NIV)

The righteous will live by faith. (Gal.3:11/NIV)

1.1. Blessings of Abraham That You Can Inherit Through Obedience

The Price Abraham had to Pay to Possess the Lord's Blessings:

The Lord had said to Abraham,
Get out of your country (*nation*),
from your people (*race*),
and from your father's house (*family*),
to a land that I will show you. (Gen. 12:1)

I. *Physical Blessings Abraham Received…*

1. I will make *you* into a great nation. (*Power & Authority*) *(Gen. 13:14-17)*

2. I will bless *you*. (*Prosperity & Security*) *(Gen.13:2; 14:23)*

3. I will make *your name* great. (*Honor & Position*) *(Gen. 14:16-20)*

4. *You* will be a blessing. (*Joy & Satisfaction in life*) *(Gen.14:16 -21)*

5. I will bless those who bless *you*. (*Many friends & Peace*) *(Gen.13:5,6)*

6. Whoever curses *you*, I will curse. (*God's curse on enemies.*) *(Gen.12:17; 14:20)*

II. *Spiritual Blessing Abraham Received…*

7. **All nations** will be blessed through you. (*through the Seed of Abraham, Jesus Christ*) (Gal.3:8, 16/NIV)

Abraham left in obedience, as the Lord had told him and Abraham and his seed inherited all the above blessings.

Obedience Brings Blessings…We too can inherit the blessings of Abraham by our obedience and faith in Jesus Christ. (Gen.12:2-4; Gal.3:14)

2. Fulfill The Law Of Christ

Commandments concerning the following topics covered in this chapter will enable you to fulfill the Law of Christ:

• Do Good To All & Reap The Harvest

• Examine Your Own Actions

*The Law of Christ...*Christ expects us to carry each other's burdens by helping needy people in times of sickness, sorrow and financial stress. When we do so, we fulfill the law of Christ. It simply means fulfilling the *second great commandment of Christ*, "You shall love your neighbor as yourself." (Matt.22:39)

Only by God's love that is poured out into our hearts through the Holy Spirit, we will be able to fulfill the law of Christ. (Rom.5:5)

*Examine Your Own Actions...*We must constantly examine our own actions and bring them in line with the Word of God and set our priorities right by putting God first in our lives. When we do this, we fulfill the *first great commandment of Christ*, "You shall love the Lord, your God with all your heart, with all your soul, and with all your mind." (Matt.22:37)

Hence, *fulfilling the law of Christ is obeying the two great commandments of Christ.* (Matt.22:37-39)

2.1. Do Good To All & Reap The Harvest

COMMANDMENTS OF GOD FOR US TO OBEY	REWARDS FOR OBEDIENCE/ CONSEQUENCES OF DISOBEDIENCE
Do good to a sinner: 1. (i) You who live by the Spirit, gently restore the one who is caught in a sin. (Gal.6:1/NIV) (ii) But watch yourself. (Gal.6:1/NIV)	i. Or you also may be tempted. (Gal.6:1/NIV) ii. If anyone *thinks* himself to be something, when he is nothing, he *deceives himself.* (Gal.6:3)
Do good to all: 2. Bear one another's burdens. (Gal.6:2)	In this way, you will *fulfill the law of Christ.* (Gal.6:2/NIV)
Do good to the family of believers: 3. Do not become weary in doing good. (Gal.6:9/NIV) 4. Do good to all people, especially to those who belong to the family of believers. (Gal.6:10/NIV)	For *at the proper time you will reap a harvest* if you do not give up. (Gal.6:9/NIV)
Do good to the one who teaches you God's Word: 5. Share all good things with your instructor. (Gal.6:6/NIV)	For the one who receives instruction in the Word should share all good things with his instructor. (Gal.6:6/NIV)

❖ *How Can We Do Good To Our Neighbors?*

Do good to your neighbors...

o By feeding those who are hungry.

o By providing clothes to the needy.

o By helping strangers, like the Good Samaritan.

o By visiting the sick.

o By visiting those in prison - as the Lord Jesus said. (Matt.25:31-46)

2.2. Be Not Deceived–God Cannot Be Mocked

Examine Your Own Actions

COMMANDMENTS OF GOD FOR US TO OBEY	REWARDS FOR OBEDIENCE/ CONSEQUENCES OF DISOBEDIENCE
1. Test your own actions. (Gal. 6:4/NIV)	Then you can *take pride in yourself alone,* without comparing yourself to someone else; for each one should carry his own load. (Gal.6:4-5/NIV)
2. Do not be deceived. (Gal.6:7)	i. For God is not mocked. (Gal.6:7)
3. Do not sow to please your flesh. (Gal.6:8/NIV)	ii. For whatever a man sows, that he will also reap. (Gal.6:7)
4. Sow to the Spirit (Holy Spirit). (Gal.6:8)	iii. Whoever sows to *please their flesh,* from the flesh will reap *destruction.* (Gal. 6:8/NIV)
	iv. But he who *sows to the Spirit* will of the Spirit reap *everlasting life.* (Gal.6:8)

- *God cannot be mocked…*Believers who *consciously* sow to please the sinful nature, the flesh, are guilty of mocking and despising God. We should not keep on *sinning, believing that God would forgive us over and over again.* If we *take God's grace in vain,* we will certainly reap destruction and death. For each of us will give an account of ourselves to God, for our every word, thought and deed, on the final Judgment Day. (Gal.6:7; Rom.6:20-23; Heb.6:4-8; 14:12; Matt.12:36; 2 Cor.5:10).

- *The Fire of God will test each one's Deeds: Your Building – Gold or Hay?* If anyone builds on the foundation (Jesus Christ) with *gold, silver,* precious stones, *wood, hay,* straw, each one's work will become clear; for the Day will declare it, because it will be revealed by fire; and the fire will *test the quality* of each one's work. If anyone's work which he has built on it endures, he will receive a *reward.* If anyone's work is burned, he will suffer *loss.* (1 Cor.3:10-15)

3. Know God Or Rather Be Known By God

COMMANDMENTS OF GOD FOR US TO OBEY	CONSEQUENCES OF DISOBEDIENCE/ SUPPORTING SCRIPTURES
1. Know God or rather be known by God.—Apostle Paul (Gal. 4:9) 2. Do not turn again to the weak and beggarly elements.—Apostle Paul. (Gal.4:9) 3. Do not observe special days and months and seasons and years. (Gal. 4:10/NIV)	Or else… i. You will serve those which *by nature are not gods.* (Gal. 4:8) ii. You will be *enslaved* by the weak and miserable forces all over again. (Gal. 4:9/NIV)

Pause & Think!

- *Know God…*You can know God by developing an intimate relationship with Jesus Christ, your Savior and by meditating the Word of God. Make Jesus your best friend by spending time with Him in prayer.

- *Be known by God…*When you walk in the fear of the true and living God, Jesus Christ, and live a life of obedience to Him, then you are known by God. You should be humble enough to be noticed by God. E.g., King David was so humble before God that he was known by God as *"the man after God's own heart."* (1 Jn.5:20; Acts 13:22)

- *This is what the Lord says*—"Israel's King and Redeemer, the Lord Almighty: I am the first and I am the last; *Apart from Me there is no God.* Who then is like Me? Let him proclaim it.

- *Is there any God besides me?* **No**, there is no other Rock; I know not one." (Is.44:6-8)

- *What are not gods by nature?*…Created things such as, *sun, moon, stars, animals, trees, mythological characters, idols* made of silver, gold, wood and stone, etc., are few examples of the things which are not gods by nature and therefore should not be worshipped as God. (Is.44:6-20)

3.1. Magic Spells & Sorceries Will Not Save You!

Our Redeemer, The LORD of Hosts, The Holy One challenges...

- "Keep on with *your magic spells* and with *your many sorceries* which you have labored at since childhood. Perhaps you will succeed, perhaps you will cause terror. (Is. 47:12)

- *All the counsel you have received has only worn you out!* (Is. 47:13)

- Let your *astrologers* come forward, those *stargazers* who make *predictions month by month,* let them save you from what is coming upon you. (Is. 47:13)

- *Surely they are like stubble,* the *fire will burn them up. They cannot even save themselves* from the power of the flame. (Is. 47:14)

- These are not coals for warmth; this is not a fire to sit by. That is all they are to you. These you have dealt with and labored with since childhood. (Is. 47:14-15)

- All of them *go on in their error;* there is *not one that can save you.*" (Is. 47:15)

❖ Warning to Those who Consult with Psychics/Mediums:

- *Statistics in USA:* Approximate number of active psychics in the US: 17,500 in 2010; 19,500 in 2015. Be Warned!

  Approximate number of people in the US who continued to consult with a psychic/medium for more than a year: 47,000 (2000-2012) and 87,000 in 2013. The number increased to 99,000 in 2014 and 145,000 in 2015. Very sad!

- *Psychics Not Communicating with God:* Unfortunately, many innocent people become victims, in their ignorance, assuming the psychics and mediums are directly communicating with God and His angels and giving them answers to their problems in life.

- **Satan Communicates with Psychics:** On the contrary, the psychics and mediums themselves are deceived by Satan and his fallen angels. Satan appears to them as the angel of light, communicates with them and deceives them, ultimately, to their own destruction.

- **Demonic Possession:** The people who consult with the psychics and mediums can be easily possessed by Satan and his demonic spirits.

3.2. To Whom Do You Go For Counsel?

- **God alone has counsel and understanding...**

The Lord God Almighty says, *"I will instruct you* and teach you in the way you should go; *I will counsel you* with My eye upon you." (Job 12:13; Ps.32:8)

- **My counsel shall stand...**(Is.46:10)

The Lord's counsel is *immutable and unchangeable.* (Heb.6:17)
The Lord is wonderful in counsel and *excellent in guidance.* (Is.28:29)

- **Whom does He counsel?**

God's secret counsel is with the **upright.** So repent of your sins, cry out to God for help and He will answer you. (Prov.3:32; Ps.121:1-2)

- **The Holy Spirit, Your Counselor...** (Jn.16:13)

The Spirit of the Lord is the *Spirit of counsel* and might. This Spirit of truth, who lives in you, will guide you into all truth. (Is.11:2)

> God is the One who has the answers to all your problems.
> His truth is what will set you free.
> **Why should you go to the world around you for counsel?**

3.3. Death–Consequence King Saul Faced When He Consulted A Medium/Psychic

Sin of Consulting a Medium/Psychic...

When King Saul saw the Philistine army, he was *afraid; terror filled his heart.* He inquired of the LORD, but the LORD did not answer him by dreams or Urim or prophets. (1 Sam.28:4-6)

Saul then said to his attendants, *"Find me a woman who is a medium,* so I may go and inquire of her." "There is one in Endor," they said. So Saul disguised himself and at night he and two men went to the woman. *"Consult a spirit for me," he said, "and bring up for me the one I name."* And she did as he requested. (1 Sam.28:7-20)

Judgment of God...

Immediately after this incident, God allowed King *Saul and his three sons to be killed in the war* against the Philistines. (1 Sam.31:1-7)

Scripture says, *"Saul died for his unfaithfulness* which he had committed against the LORD, because he did not keep the word of the LORD, and also *because he consulted a medium for guidance.* But he did not inquire of the LORD, therefore He killed him, and turned the kingdom over to David." (1 Chr.10:13-14)

King Saul did not truly repent of his sins nor did he humble himself and seek the Lord wholeheartedly. He did not wait on the Lord until he heard from Him. God was gracious to King Saul though he had disobeyed God's commandments in the past. But when he took the counsel from the witch, *he crossed the line of God's grace* and the judgment of God came upon him. Very sad!

Lessons to Learn...

- Do **not seek the counsel of a medium/psychic.** They cannot help you but may bring the judgment of God upon you.

- **Abomination to the Lord...** All those who practice witchcraft and sorcery, those who call upon the dead, and those who go to a medium are an abomination to the Lord. The Lord your God has **not appointed such for you.** (Deut.18:10-14)

❖ Do Not Practice Witchcraft Against Fellow Believers:

- It is the responsibility of the teachers of God's Word to **instruct people not to practice witchcraft or go to psychics for counselling** but rather turn to God in times of need; so that we do not transgress the commandment of God. (Matt.15:3, 6-9)

- No one should dare to do witchcraft, i.e. sending demonic spirits, especially against a fellow believer in Christ, to destroy his life. Surely, God's judgment will come upon him.

- When the evil forces come against you, *resist them in Jesus' Name, by declaring,*

   i. "Surely there is **no magic curse** against Jacob; **no divination** against Israel." (Num.23:23)
   ii. **"No weapon** formed against us shall prosper." (Is.54:17)

- Overcome Satan and his hosts by the **Blood of the Lamb, Jesus,** and by the word of your testimony. (Rev.12:11)

4. No Longer You Live, But Christ Lives In You

*Intimacy with Christ...*Those who have faith in Christ should live their lives in intimate union with their Lord, both in His death and resurrection. (Rom.6:3-5)

*Our old self crucified with Christ...*As a true believer, you are crucified with Christ on the cross. Sin will no longer have control over you and you no longer live but Christ lives in you. (Rom.6:6,14; Gal.5:24)

*Walk in newness of life in Christ...*You who have been crucified with Christ, now live with Him in His resurrection. ***Christ's power is available to you to make you an overcomer of sin.*** It is through the Holy Spirit that Christ's risen life is continuously operating in you. Those who are united with Christ in His death and resurrection are freed from sin's power to walk in newness of life. (Jn.14-16; Rom.6:1-12; 8:10-11; Acts1:8)

*Being transformed from glory to glory in the image of Christ...*Jesus simply stated that after we are born again, we should *daily deny ourselves, take up our cross* and *follow Him.* As believers, when we abide in Christ, we are being transformed into the same image of Christ, from glory to glory, by the Spirit of the Lord. It took Apostle Paul several years to say, "I have been crucified with Christ; it is no longer I who live, but Christ lives in me." (Lk.9:23; 2 Cor.3:18; Gal.2:20)

*You are made alive in Christ...*You *reckon yourselves to be dead indeed to sin* but alive to God in Christ Jesus our Lord. Once you accept Christ, your mindset must be changed how you perceive sin and eventually you will be able to overcome sin by the power of the Holy Spirit. (Rom.6:11; Eph.2:5)

* *After many years of walking with the Lord in the narrow path, finally, I can say now, I know the Lord Jesus, my Bridegroom, to be...*

- *100% Loving*

- *100% Caring*

- *100% Forgiving*

- *100% Gracious*

- *100% Merciful*

- *100% Compassionate*

- *100% Holy*

- *100% Righteous*

- *100% God of Justice, when it comes to sin. (Acts 5:1-10; Deut.28:15-68)*

*There is no favoritism with the Lord, especially when it comes to chastisement for sin. **When much is given to you, much is expected of you.** This applies to all believers, especially to the Servants of God. (Hos.2:19-20; Rom.2:11; Lk.12:48; Jn.14:21-23; 2 Sam.11-19; Acts 10:34) – Author*

❖ **Commandments on the following topics in this chapter will help you to "Die to Self" and walk in the newness of life in Christ....**

- How does Christ live in you?

- How to be crucified with Christ?

- How to be dead to sin?

- How to be crucified to the world?

- How to live a New Life?

4.1. How Does Christ Live In You?

COMMANDMENTS OF GOD FOR US TO OBEY	REWARDS FOR OBEDIENCE/ SUPPORTING SCRIPTURES
1. Be crucified with Christ, as apostle Paul was. (Gal.2:20)	i. Then it is no longer you who live, but *Christ lives in you.* ii. The life which you now live in the flesh, you *live by faith in the Son of God*, who loved you and gave Himself for you. (Gal.2:20)
2. *Crucify the sinful nature* with its passions and desires. (Gal.5:24/NIV) 3. Let us not become conceited, provoking and envying each other. (Gal.5:26/NIV)	For those who *belong to Christ* have crucified the sinful nature with its passions and desires. (Gal.5:24/NIV)

- *Crucified with Christ…Now if we died with Christ, we will also live with Him.* If we have been united with Christ in His death, we will certainly be united with Him in His resurrection. (Rom.6:5,8)

  Apostle Paul explains that crucifying your sinful nature is an ongoing process because your spirit which has been crucified and died with Christ, still resides within the flesh which is very much alive. (Rom.7:18-25)

- *The Holy Spirit enables you to crucify the flesh…*You cannot overcome your inherited sinful nature on your own but you need the power and guidance of the Holy Spirit to die to "Self." The Holy Spirit changes you from producing the deeds of the flesh to producing the fruit of the Spirit. (Rom.8:2)

- *Christ lives in you…*When Christ lives in you, His Power is within you, becoming the source of all of life and the center of all your thoughts, words and deeds. (Jn.15:1-6)

- *Live by faith in the Son of God…*Those who put their faith in Christ will live their lives in *intimate union with their Lord Jesus Christ; for Christ is the True God and Eternal Life.* (1 Jn.5:20)

4.1(a) Only Your Spirit Transformed At Salvation

When you accept Christ into your heart by faith, the following changes take place in your spirit –

1. You are *saved by the grace* of Jesus Christ. (Eph.2:8-9)

2. You receive the *free gift of salvation*. (Eph.2:8-9)

3. You are *forgiven* of all your past sins at salvation. (1 Jn.1:9; Acts 2:38)

4. You are *redeemed* through Christ. (Eph.1:7)

5. You are *sanctified* by Christ. (Heb.10:10; 1 Cor.1:2)

6. You become a *child of God* once you are saved. (Gal.3:26)

7. You are a *new creature in Christ*. (2 Cor.5:17)

8. You are made *righteous* in Christ, in your spirit. (1 Cor.1:30)

9. You are *justified* by putting your faith in Christ. (Gal.2:16-17)

10. You are *born again,* in your spirit, at the time of salvation. (Jn.3:3)

11. You are *made alive* in Christ. (Eph.2:5)

12. You are a *saint* in Christ. (Rom.1:7; 8:27; 2 Thes.1:10)

4.1(b) Our Spirit, Soul & Body Saved –
By Grace & Obedience

I. Only Your Spirit, Saved by God's Grace

- When you accept Christ as your Savior, only your spirit becomes righteous, by His grace. You are *saved, forgiven, redeemed, sanctified, made righteous,* etc. – all these changes happen *only in your spirit man*, at salvation. (1Cor.1:30; 2 Cor.5:17, 21; Eph.1:7; 2:5, 8, 9; 1 Jn.1:9; Heb.10:10; James 1:18)

- Scripture says, The "Gift of Righteousness" reigns in our life through Christ. Therefore, *righteousness is a gift to our "spirit."* (Rom.3:21-24; 5:17)

- Jesus loves you enough that He died on the cross, in your place, to redeem you from eternal Hell-fire. Don't you want to please this loving Jesus at any cost? (Is.53:5; Jn.3:36; 11:25, 26)

II. Your Soul, Saved by God's Word

i. Your *soul is being saved* by the renewing of your mind with the Word of God all through your life. You should take captive every thought to make it *obedient* to Christ. (James 1:21; Rom.12:1-2; 2 Cor.10:5)

ii. Your soul is *earthly, sensual and demonic* or open to the demonic realm. Hence, your soul needs to be saved and transformed by the Word of truth. (James 3:15; Rom.12:1-2)

iii. Your soul or mind and your body become righteous by obedience to the commandments of God, every day of your life. (Rom.6:13; Matt.5:20)

III. Your Body, Saved by Obeying God's Commandments

- Your body, the *flesh*, with its sinful nature, must be crucified daily on the cross. Jesus says, *Deny yourself, take up your cross* and follow Me;

for narrow is the path that leads to Eternal Life. (Gal.5:19-21; 2:20; Lk.9:23; Matt.7:14)

- We must **guard our salvation with fear and trembling,** by obeying the commandments of God. Only those who endure till the end shall be saved. (Phil.2:12; Matt.24:13; Jn.14:15; Rom.6:6; Matt.28:18-20)

- We cannot say that we accept Jesus but reject His Word, His commandments. For Jesus Himself declared, "Why do you call Me 'Lord, Lord,' and **not do the things which I say?**" (Lk.6:46-49; Matt.7:21-27)

- "God shows no partiality. In every nation whoever fears Him and **works righteousness** is accepted by Him." You can work righteousness by obeying His commands. (Acts 10:34, 35; Matt.5:20)

- **Be an Overcomer:** As New Testament believers in Christ, we should **overcome 100% of sin (flesh), world and Satan;** for the Overcomers will receive eternal rewards in Heaven. (Rev.2-3)

    i. Sin shall not have dominion over you, since you are not under law (OT) but under grace (NT). (Rom.6:14)

    ii. **Do not love the world or anything in the world;** for all that is in the world, the lust of the flesh, the lust of the eyes, and the pride of life - is not of the Father, but of the world. Friendship with the world is enmity against God. (Jn.17:16; 1Jn.2:15-17; James 4:4)

    iii. Jesus disarmed the principalities and the powers of darkness, triumphing over Satan by the cross; and Jesus says, "I have given you authority to trample on snakes and scorpions and to **overcome all the power of the enemy;** nothing will harm you." (Col.2:15; Lk.10:19)

    iv. **Bind the strongman, Satan,** and take back everything he has stolen from you; Overcome Satan by the Blood of the Lamb, Jesus, and by the word of your testimony. (Matt.12:29; Rev.12:11)

    v. Put on the whole armor of God, and **wrestle against principalities,** against powers, against rulers of darkness of this world, against spiritual wickedness in high places - which come against your family, your city and nation. (Eph.6:11-17)

    vi. If you are 100% obedient to God, the **God of peace will soon crush Satan under your feet.** (Rom.16:20)

IV. God's Way, Not Our Way

Jesus did the Supernatural (Grace) to redeem our spirit man and *we need to do the Natural (Obedience)* to crucify our flesh on the cross, with the help of the Holy Spirit of God, our Helper, made available to us by Christ Himself. Jesus has done His part and He expects us to do our part. That is God's way! God's ways are always higher than our ways. (Eph.1:19-23; Jn.14:15-17; Rom.8:26-27; Is.55:8-9)

V. Jesus Promises Another Helper - To Obey His Commands

• *"If you love Me, **obey My commandments.** And I will pray the Father, and He will **give you another Helper,** that He may abide with you forever -* You know Him, for He dwells with you and will be in you." – Jesus. (Jn.14:15-17)

• Jesus, not only asked us to obey His commandments but also has sent us another ***Helper, the Holy Spirit of God,** to enable us to obey His commandments,* all the days of our lives. This is the Grace of God! (Rom.1:5)

VI. Total Salvation of Your Spirit, Soul & Body

Grace and Obedience go together. They are like two sides of the same coin. In fact, through Christ, we receive grace even for obedience. Hence, Grace of Christ and Obedience to God's Commandments, both are required for the *total salvation of your spirit, soul and body.* (Rom.1:5; Lk.6:46; Matt.7:21-27; Acts 10:35; Matt.5:20)

4.2. How To Be Crucified With Christ?

COMMANDMENTS OF GOD FOR US TO OBEY	REWARDS FOR OBEDIENCE/ SUPPORTING SCRIPTURES
1. Count yourselves *dead to sin* but alive to God in Christ Jesus. (Rom.6:11/NIV; Gal.2:20; 5:24)	i. *For sin shall not be your master,* because you are not under law, but *under grace.* (Rom.6:14/NIV)
2. Do not let sin reign in your mortal body so that you obey its evil desires. (Rom.6:12/NIV)	ii. *If Christ is in you, the body is dead because of sin,* but the Spirit *is* life because of righteousness. (Rom.8:10)
3. Do not offer the parts of your body to sin, as instruments of wickedness; but rather offer yourselves to God. (Rom.6:13/NIV)	iii. For our old man was *crucified with Christ,* that the body of sin might be done away with, that *we should no longer be slaves of sin.* (Rom.6:6)
4. *Offer every part of yourself to God as an instrument of righteousness.* *(Rom.6:13/NIV)*	iv. For he who has died has been *freed from sin.* (Rom.6:7)

★ *At every stage of my spiritual training, the Lord would ask me, "Are you ready to go in the path of your Redeemer? For it is a path of suffering." And every time I said, "Yes, Lord!" It has been an extremely tough path so far, but the Lord has graciously brought the best out of me.*

The Lord will purify us and bring the gold out of us, by taking us through the cave of afflictions. – Author

4.3. How to be Dead to Sin?

It is impossible to be dead to sin except by the Holy Spirit...

- *Through the Holy Spirit...*You cannot be dead to sin in your own strength. But you can overcome your flesh when you totally depend on the power of the Holy Spirit; for the **Lord is that Spirit.** (2 Cor.3:17) The more the Holy Spirit of God fills you with the glory of God and empowers your inner man, the more you will be dead to sin.

- *Through the Son, Jesus...* If the Son sets you free, you will be free indeed. Through Christ, the Spirit who gives life will set you *free from the law of sin* and death. (Jn.8:36; Rom.8:2/NIV)

- *By the Fullness of Christ...You should be filled with the fullness of Christ (100 %)* to be dead to sin. (Eph. 4:13)

- *The extent to which you allow Christ* to live in you, to the *same extent* you will be dead to sin. (Rom.8:10)

- *How to be filled with the Fullness of Christ?* Know the love of Christ which passes knowledge; so that you may be filled with *all the fullness of God.* (Eph. 3:17-19; 4:13)

It is a process through which God will take you until you are filled with the fullness of Christ. As you yield to the Spirit of God and *wait on the Lord* in the Most Holy Place, you will be filled with His Glory, i.e., the fullness of Christ.—*From Author's Experience.*

⋆   *The Lord, in His grace, has helped me to forsake my all for Christ. I have paid a very heavy price for my calling. Since 1992, the Lord started giving me choices - Jesus or my job, Jesus or the comforts of this world, Jesus or worldly fame, honor and prosperity that would have come through my medical profession. Only by God's grace, I could choose Jesus over all the above choices.*

   The Lord keeps testing us and scoring us for our Heavenly rewards. Nothing we sacrifice on earth for Christ, will go without rewards.- Author

4.4. How To Be Crucified To The World?

You are crucified to the world only through Christ.

COMMANDMENTS OF GOD FOR US TO OBEY	REWARDS FOR OBEDIENCE/ SUPPORTING SCRIPTURES
1. *Never boast except in the Cross* of our Lord Jesus Christ, as apostle Paul stated. (Gal.6:14/NIV)	i. For *only through Christ, the world is crucified to you* and you to the world, as it was for apostle Paul. (Gal.6.14) ii. For it is *by grace you have been saved,* through faith—and this not of yourselves, it is the *gift of God—not by works, so that no one can boast.* (Eph.2:8-9) iii. As many as *walk according to this rule, peace and mercy be* upon them, and *upon the Israel* of God. (Gal.6:16)
2. Do not subject yourself to the regulations (ways) of the world. (Col. 2:20/NIV)	i. *For you have died with Christ* to the basic principles of this world. ii. If you submit to the rules of the world, it is as though *you still belong to the world*. (Col.2:20/NIV)
3. Do not submit to the rules of the world - "Do not handle! Do not taste! Do not touch!" which are based on merely *human commands and teachings*. (Col. 2:21-22/NIV)	i. For these rules have to do with things that are *all destined to perish with use.* (Col. 2:22/NIV) ii. For such regulations indeed have an appearance of wisdom, with their self-imposed worship, their false humility and their harsh treatment of the body, but *they lack any value in restraining sensual indulgence.* (Col. 2:23/NIV)

4.5. How To Live A New Life?

COMMANDMENTS OF GOD FOR US TO OBEY	REWARDS FOR OBEDIENCE/ SUPPORTING SCRIPTURES
1. *Be baptized into Christ's death.* (Rom. 6:3) 2. *Be buried with Christ* through *baptism* into His death. (Rom. 6:4/NIV)	So that, just as Christ was raised from the dead *through the glory of the Father, we too may live a new life.* (Rom.6:4/NIV)
3. Be baptized into Christ. (Gal.3:27; Rom.6:3)	For you will **put on Christ.** (Gal.3:27)

- It is **only through the Holy Spirit,** Christ's risen life will manifest in you. (Jn.16:13-14)

* *For more details on "How to live a new life," please refer to* **chapter 2 in the Book of Ephesians in this book.**

❖ *In order* **to die 100% to sin, flesh & the world,** *a believer should consider himself to be...*

1. **Crucified with Christ.** (Gal.2:20)

2. **Dead with Christ.** (Col.2:20)

3. **Baptized into Christ's death.** (Rom.6:3)

4. **Buried with Christ** through baptism into His death. (Rom.6:4)

5. **United with Christ** in His death. (Rom.6:5)

6. **United with Christ in His resurrection.** (Rom.6:5)

7. **Risen with Christ.** (Col.3:1)

8. **Seated with Christ** in the heavenly realms. (Eph.2:6)

When you are crucified, baptized into Christ's death and buried with Christ, you will be totally dead to sin (100%) and sin will not have dominion over you. (Rom.6:1-14)

Holy Spirit, Your Helper...You don't need to strive to be crucified with Christ to die to self. But as you yield to the Holy Spirit and remain still in His Presence, you will eventually be transformed into the likeness of Christ.—*From Author's Experience*

Now, if you died with Christ, you will also live with Him. Then you can be an overcomer and receive the rewards of an overcomer in Heaven. (Rom.6:8; Rev.2-3)

❖ *The Holy Spirit Anoints You...*

o   When you wait on God with hunger. (Acts 2:1-4; Jn.7:37-38)

o   When you praise God rejoicingly. (Lk.1:67-68; Lk.10:21)

o   When you worship God. (Eph.5:18-20; Acts 16:25-26; Jn.4:23-24)

o   When you meditate the Word of God. (Acts 2:14-38; Acts 11:15-17)

o   When you pray in the Spirit. (Rom.8:26-27; Acts 2:1-4; 4:31)

o   When you serve God. (Acts 11:15-17; 19:1-7; Heb.13:21)

o   When you preach the Word. (Acts 2:14-40; 11:15-17)

o   When you obey God's Commands. (Jn.14:15-17)

o   When you give unto God cheerfully. (Acts 10:1-6)

o   When you die to "Self." (Gal.2:20; 5:16-21, 24-25; Lk.9:23)

★   *In the year 1992, the Lord asked me, "I died on the cross for you, what have you done for Me? Will you serve me until you have your last breath? Will you follow Me to do My ministry?" I immediately responded, "Yes, Lord but first my job." That was the beginning of my calling. The "Dying to Self" process started from then on. Jesus enrolled me in His school of training and prepared me first, before calling me into full time ministry.*

It looked like the Lord wanted to know how much price I would be willing to pay, whether I would lay down my lucrative Medical career on the altar, in order to follow Him. I did it with great difficulty, against all odds.

In 1995, the Lord promised me, "Since you were precious in My sight, you have been **honored** *(with this high calling), and I have loved you; therefore* **I will give men for your life.**" *(Is.43:4) Jesus has been faithful in fulfilling this promise. – Author*

5. Teachers Of God's Word

*Teachers, Appointed by God...*Scripture says, "To each one of us grace was given according to the measure of Christ's gift. And Christ Himself gave some to be *apostles,* some *prophets,* some evangelists, and some pastors and *teachers, for the equipping of the saints for the work of ministry,* for the edifying of the body of Christ. (Eph.4:11-12)

*Main Duties...*It is the responsibility of the Teachers of God's Word to *make every believer a perfect man*; filled with the knowledge of the Son of God and the *fullness of Christ*. (Col.1:28)

The Lord Jesus says to the Teachers of God's Word, *"What I tell you in the dark* (early morning hours), speak in the daylight; *what is whispered in your ear,* proclaim from the roofs." (Matt.10:27)

*Hear from the Lord & Preach...*Wait on the Lord until you receive the Word from Him. Then the message you preach will be more anointed and appropriate to the people who hear it. The Word of God you teach will convict them to change their wrong ways and be 100% fruitful for the Kingdom of God; for the Lord only knows what kind of situation people are in.

If you do not hear from the Lord and preach the "Word" in the flesh, it may produce only 30 or 60 fold fruit in peoples' lives. Your effort will not bring fullness of God's blessings to people and your rewards in heaven also will be limited.

5.1. Do Not Distort The Gospel Of Christ

The Gospel of Christ is the good news of salvation that comes through faith, by the grace of Jesus Christ, who died in our place, rose again and is still alive. (Eph.2:8-9; 1 Thess.4:14)

COMMANDMENTS OF GOD FOR US TO OBEY	CONSEQUENCES OF DISOBEDIENCE
1. Do not turn away from God who called you in the grace of Christ, to a different gospel - Apostle Paul. (Gal.1:6) 2. Do not pervert the gospel of Christ.—Apostle Paul. (Gal.1:7) 3. Do not preach the gospel according to man; but *by the revelation of Jesus Christ,* as Apostle Paul did. (Gal.1:11-12)	i. If *we, or an angel* from heaven, preach any other gospel to you, other than the gospel of Christ, let him be *accursed* – Apostle Paul. (Gal.1:8) ii. If *anyone* preaches any other gospel to you, other than the gospel of Christ, let him be *under God's curse* – Apostle Paul. (Gal.1:9/NIV)

*Do not pervert the Gospel of Christ…*Apostle Paul cautions the teachers of God's Word not to turn to a different gospel which is not a gospel at all, but preach the good news only by the revelation of Jesus Christ, as he did.

In these last days, many are distorting the truth of the Gospel of Christ, confusing the innocent and the new believers. Paul warns that if anyone preaches the gospel other than the Gospel of Jesus Christ, *he will be under God's curse.* (Gal.1:7-12/NIV)

5.2. Do Not Try To Win The Approval Of Men

Jesus said to the Pharisees, "You are the ones who justify yourselves in the eyes of men, but God knows your hearts. *For what is highly valued among men is detestable in God's sight.*" (Lk.16:15)

COMMANDMENTS OF GOD FOR US TO OBEY	CONSEQUENCES OF DISOBEDIENCE
1. Do not persuade men but God – Apostle Paul. (Gal.1:10) 2. Do not try to please men - Apostle Paul. (Gal.1:10/NIV)	For if you please men, you will *not be a servant of Christ – Apostle Paul.* (Gal.1:10/NIV)
3. Do not be highly esteemed among men. (Lk.16:15)	For it is *an abomination* in the sight of God. (Lk.16:15)

- *For more commandments on this topic, please read Chapter 26 "**Teachers of God's Word**" in my first book titled "All the Commandments of God" Volume I.*

* *"**Cast your burden only on Me** and not on any human being," the Lord often says to me.*

When we put this into practice - it shows to God that we totally depend on Him (100%). It is an ongoing process. The sooner we learn, the better it is for us. Little by little we learn to take our eyes off of human beings and trust only Jesus. Jesus, our possessive Bridegroom expects this from His Bride, the Church. – Author

5.3. Be A Servant Of God Like Apostle Paul

*Apostle Paul, not a men-pleaser...*When Paul had the call directly from the Lord Jesus to preach the gospel among the gentiles, *he did not consult any man,* nor did he go up to Jerusalem to see Peter, James and John, who were apostles before him. He did not seek their approval to do the Lord's will for his life. (Gal.1:16-17)

Apostle Paul was not swayed by people of position and power. For he says, "As for *those who seem to be important - whatever they were, makes no difference to me; God shows personal favoritism to no man.* (Gal. 2:6/NIV)

*Apostle Paul, a man of Prayer...*Paul went immediately into Arabia and spent time alone with God. It was a time of preparation for Apostle Paul for the great ministry ahead among the gentiles. (Gal.1:18)

Apostle Paul, a God-pleaser... After three years in Arabia, Paul went up to Jerusalem to see Peter and stayed with him for fifteen days. *Then after fourteen years only,* he went up again to Jerusalem *by revelation of God* and communicated with Peter and the other disciples about how he ministered among the gentiles and that he had not been running his race in vain. (Gal.1:18-24; 2:1-2)

Apostle Paul was totally dependent on God for guidance and fulfilled God's perfect will for his life. For he says, "Am I now trying to win the approval of human beings, or of God? *If I were still trying to please people, I would not be a servant of Christ."* (Gal.1:10)

*Be a God-pleaser and not a men-pleaser...*Once you become a believer, you should make all efforts to please only God even if it means displeasing your friends, family members and people of position and power.

6. Unity—You Are All One In Christ Jesus

COMMANDMENTS OF GOD FOR US TO OBEY	REWARDS FOR OBEDIENCE/ SUPPORTING SCRIPTURES
You all be one in Christ Jesus— Apostle Paul. (Gal.3:28/NIV)	1. For in Christ, there is neither Jew nor Greek, neither *slave* nor free, neither *male nor female.* (Gal.3:28) 2. For as many of you as were baptized into Christ have *put on Christ.* (Gal.3:27)

Pause & Think!

- *Put on Christ...*Apostle Paul states that there are no ethnic, national, linguistic, socio economic and gender barriers **when you have intimate relationship with the Lord Jesus Christ.**

- **Christ's heart must be bleeding to see us divided** and diverted from our God-given destiny. We are blinded by our superstitions, rituals, traditions, doctrines and various denominations, thereby causing great damage to the Body of Christ.

- The only thing that matters is that **we are all bought by the priceless Blood** of our Lord Jesus. Remember, Christ is our Head and we are the different members of His Body, regardless of who we are. So let us be united in Christ, irrespective of our race, color, creed, gender, language, nationality, social status, etc. (Eph.5:30)

Who Divides Us?

From the beginning of creation, Satan has been using the same strategy *"divide and conquer"* to destroy the human race. Satan is always at work. Remember, Satan never takes a vacation. We must not be ignorant of Satan's schemes. (2 Cor.2:11)

United We Stand, Divided We Fall!

7. Your Spirit In Conflict With The Flesh

*Spirit against the flesh...*The flesh desires what is contrary to the Spirit and the Spirit desires what is contrary to the sinful nature, the flesh. They are in conflict with each other. (Gal.5:17)

Walk by the Spirit and you will not gratify the desires of the flesh. (Gal.5:16)

Those who are Christ's have crucified the flesh with its passions and desires. (Gal.5:1, 24)

COMMANDMENTS OF GOD FOR US TO OBEY	CONSEQUENCES OF DISOBEDIENCE
1. Do not practice the "works of the flesh." (Gal. 5:19-21)	For those who practice the works of the flesh will **not inherit the Kingdom of God.** (Gal. 5:19-21)
2. Do not conduct yourselves in the lusts of your flesh, fulfilling the desires of the flesh and of the mind.—Apostle Paul. (Eph.2:3)	Or else, you will be *"children of wrath, just as the others."*—Apostle Paul. (Eph.2:3)

Points to Ponder:

- If you are led by the Spirit, you are not under the law. (Gal.5:18)

- If we live in the Spirit, let us also walk in the Spirit. (Gal.5:25)

- *Accountable to God?* All our "Self" promoting words, thoughts and deeds are being *recorded (audio & video)* in the spiritual realm and will be taken against us on the final Judgment Day. (Rev.20:12)

- *The Great White Throne Judgment:* In the Book of Revelation, Apostle John writes, "I saw a great white throne and Him (Christ) who sat on it. I saw the dead, small and great, standing before God, and **books were opened** and the *dead were judged according to their works,* by the things which were **written in the books."** (Rev.20:11-15)

7.1. The Unrighteous Will Not Inherit The Kingdom of God

I. *The Works of the Flesh*

1. Adultery
2. Fornication
3. Uncleanness
4. Licentiousness (recklessness)
5. Idolatry
6. *Sorcery*
7. *Hatred*
8. *Contentions (strife)*
9. Jealousies
10. Outburst of *wrath*
11. *Selfish ambitions*
12. Dissensions (rebellion)
13. Heresies
14. *Envy*
15. Murders
16. *Drunkenness*
17. Revelries (wild partying) and those who practice such things will *not inherit the kingdom of God.* (Gal.5:19-21)

II. *Do Not Be Deceived*

Neither fornicators, *nor adulterers,*
nor homosexuals, nor sodomites,
nor idolaters,
nor thieves, nor extortioners,
nor covetous,
nor drunkards, nor revilers will inherit the kingdom of God. (1 Cor.6:9-10)

8. You Are Not Under Law But Under Grace

Christ has redeemed us from the curse of the law, having become a curse for us; for it is written, "Cursed is everyone who hangs on a tree." (Gal.3:13)

The word "Law" (Heb. Torah) means "teaching or direction."

Three Divisions of Law... The Law of God given to Moses can be divided into 3 categories:

1. *The moral law* deals with God's standards for holy living. (Ex.20:1-17)
2. *The civil law* deals with Israel's legal and social life. (Ex.21–23)
3. *The ceremonial law* deals with the form and ritual of Israel's worship of the Lord, including the sacrificial system. (Lev.1-19)

What was the purpose of the law? (Gal. 3:19)

Is the law against the promises of God? Certainly not! (Gal. 3:21)

The law was added because of transgressions until the Seed, Jesus Christ had come to whom the promise was made. It brings unconscious sin into consciousness and makes people actual transgressors. (Gal. 3:19)

*Conviction of sin...*The law convicted people of sin until Jesus Christ came but after Christ, the Holy Spirit of God in us convicts us of sin. (Gal.3:19; Jn.16:8)

8.1. You Are Redeemed From The Law Through Christ

Christ declared, "Do not think that I came to destroy the Law or the Prophets. *I did not come to destroy but to fulfill.*

For assuredly, I say to you, till heaven and earth pass away, *one jot or one tittle will by no means pass from the law till all is fulfilled."* (Matt.5:17-18)

Jesus fulfilled the sacrificial and ceremonial laws at the cross, by becoming the Lamb of atonement that was slain once for all, to redeem us from our sins and from the law. So, now salvation comes only by grace through faith in Jesus Christ and not by observing these sacrificial and ceremonial laws (OT). (Gal.3:19; Heb.10:10; Eph.2:8-9)

Jesus obeyed the moral law by leading a sinless life on earth. Jesus fulfilling the moral law does not mean that we do not need to obey the moral law (OT). The moral law, i.e. the commandments of God, which deals with God's standard of righteousness is still applicable to us today. *These laws are not for our salvation* but they will help our spiritual growth and enable us to live a righteous life. (Heb.4:15; Ex.20:1-17)

So when Paul says, "You are redeemed from the law," what he means is that *we must not view the law* as a system of legal commandments *for our Salvation.* For salvation comes only through faith in Jesus Christ. (Rom.10:9)

I. *The Laws that the Believer is Obligated to Keep Include;*

• The ethical and moral principles of the OT.
• The teachings of Christ and the Apostles.

These laws reveal God's moral nature and His will for His people and, therefore still apply today. By obeying them, we express the life of Christ in us.

II. *The Laws that No Longer Apply to the Believers:*

The OT Laws that apply directly to the nation of Israel, such as...

- Sacrificial Law (Lev.1-19)

- Ceremonial Law or ritual (e.g., circumcision) (Heb.10:1-10)

- Social Law relates to Israel's social life.

- Civil Law which deals with Israel's legal system.

COMMANDMENT OF GOD FOR US TO OBEY	REWARDS FOR OBEDIENCE
Redemption in Jesus:	*For Believers:*
Be redeemed from the law through God's Son, Jesus Christ – Apostle Paul. (Gal.4:4-5,7)	1. So that you might receive the **adoption as sons.** (Gal.4:5)
	2. Because you are sons, God sent the **Spirit of His Son into your hearts,** the Spirit who calls out, Abba, Father. (Gal.4:6/NIV)
	3. You are **no more a servant,** but a son. (Gal.4:7/KJV)
	4. Since you are a son, God has made you also **an heir** through Christ. (Gal.4:7/NIV)

- *This commandment of God applies to the unbelieving gentiles.*

The Moral Law of God -
10 COMMANDMENTS

I THOU SHALT HAVE
NO OTHER GODS
BEFORE ME

II THOU SHALT NOT
MAKE UNTO THEE
ANY GRAVEN IMAGE

III THOU SHALT NOT
TAKE THE NAME
OF THE LORD THY
GOD IN VAIN

IV REMEMBER THE
SABBATH DAY,
TO KEEP IT HOLY

V HONOUR THY FATHER
AND THY MOTHER

VI THOU SHALT
NOT KILL

VII THOU SHALT NOT
COMMIT ADULTERY

VIII THOU SHALT
NOT STEAL

IX THOU SHALT NOT
BEAR FALSE
WITNESS AGAINST
THY NEIGHBOUR

X THOU SHALT
NOT COVET

8.2. Why Should We Obey The Old Testament Moral Laws?

- **Commandments, Prophecies & Promises of God**...The moral law i.e., the commandments of God, the prophecies concerning the Second Coming of Christ and the promises of God in the Old Testament, all will be fulfilled, even to the jot and tittle, till heaven and earth pass away, as Jesus declared. (Matt.5:17-18)

- Jesus Himself states that **God's commandment is life everlasting.** (Jn.12:50)

- **If Christ has upgraded** the commandments in the Old Testament then we should obey His upgraded commandments. The commandments which are not upgraded by Jesus will remain as they are and must be obeyed.

- **Obedience to the least of God's Commandments**...Jesus also stated that whoever breaks one of the least of God's commandments, and teaches men so, shall be called least in the kingdom of heaven; but whoever does and teaches them, he shall be called **great in the kingdom of heaven.** (Matt.5:19)

- **Jesus Counsels the Rich Young Ruler and affirms the need to obey God's Commandments....**

    A rich young ruler came to Jesus and said, "Good Teacher, **what good thing shall I do that I may have eternal life?"**

    Jesus said to him, "**If you want to enter into life, keep the Commandments."**

    The rich young ruler asked Jesus, "Which ones?" Jesus replied, "'You shall not murder,' 'You shall not commit adultery,' 'You shall not steal,' 'You shall not bear false witness,' 'Honor your father and *your* mother,' and, 'You shall love your neighbor as yourself.' " (Matt.19:16-19)

    In Matthew 19:16, Jesus was asked what must be done to inherit eternal life. Jesus then listed several of the Ten Commandments from the Old Testament to the rich young ruler, thereby emphasizing that we need to obey God's commandments.

- *Importance of Obeying the Commandments of God mentioned in the Book of Revelation...*

In Rev.12:13-17, Satan or the dragon, who deceives the whole world when he was cast to the earth went to make war with those who **keep the commandments of God** and hold fast their testimony of *Jesus*.

Again, Rev.14:12 mentions about the patience of the saints who **keep the commandments of God** and the faith of Jesus.

Amazingly, **the Book of Revelation,** the last book in the Bible, emphasizes that we, believers in Christ, should *obey both* the Commandments of God (OT) and Commandments of Christ (NT). (Rev.12:17; 14:12; 22:14)

Knowledge about the moral commandments of God from the OT and NT is extremely important so that the Holy Spirit can convict us when we break the Commandments and make us righteous in our soul and body, as we obey them. (Jn.14:15-17)

- *You can obey the Commandments of God only by the power of the Holy Spirit...*

In the Old Testament, people obeyed the commandments of God out of fear of God and of His judgments. (Ex.19; 20:1-17; 32; Num.21:4-10)

But in the New Covenant, we should obey the commandments out of love for God. After Christ came, the power of the Holy Spirit is available to help us obey the commandments of God. The Holy Spirit working within us empowers us to live a righteous life before God. (Jn.14:15-17)

8.3. Relying On The Works Of The Law For Our Salvation Brings A Curse

1. *"Is the Law sin? Certainly not...* Indeed I would not have known what sin was except through the Law." For example, "I would not have known what coveting really was if the Law had not said, 'Do not covet.'" (Rom.7:7)

2. And I found out that my spirit was dead because of my sin. "Therefore *the Law is holy and the commandment holy and just and good.* Was then that which is good made *death unto me?* God forbid!" (Rom.7:12-13)

   "We know that the *Law is spiritual* but we are carnal sold under sin." states apostle Paul. (Rom.7:14)

3. Apostle Paul also says, *I delight in the Law* of God in my inner being. So then, with the mind *I myself serve the law of God,* but with the flesh the law of sin. (Rom.7:22,25)

4. Hence, we believers should no longer look to the OT Law and sacrifices for our salvation and acceptance from God. Apostle Paul states that *if we look to the law for our salvation, then we are under a curse.*

5. Now that we are united to Christ, we should *look to Christ for our salvation.* Since *Christ has fulfilled the ceremonial and the sacrificial law* at the cross, if we still follow these laws for our salvation, we will be under a curse. (Gal.3:10)

6. The law is not of faith, but the man who does them (i.e. commandments) *shall live by them.* (Gal.3:12)

7. Grace and obedience to the moral law, i.e. the commandments of God are not in conflict, for they both point to righteousness and holiness. (Rom.7:12-13)

COMMANDMENTS OF GOD FOR US TO OBEY	CONSEQUENCES OF DISOBEDIENCE/ SUPPORTING SCRIPTURES
1. Do not rely on the works of the law (*ceremonial & sacrificial law*). (Gal.3:10/NIV)	1. *For all who rely* on the works of the law are *under a curse.* (Gal.3:10/NIV)
	2. "*Cursed* is everyone who does not continue to do *everything* written in the Book of the Law." (Gal.3:10/NIV; Deut. 27:26)
	3. *No one is justified* by the law in the sight of God. (Gal. 3:11)
	4. The law cannot annul the covenant that was confirmed to Abraham by God in Christ. (Gal. 3:16-17)
	5. For your inheritance is not of the law but by the promise of God in Christ. (Gal.3:18)
	6. There is *no law that could impart life.* (Gal.3:21)
	7. Righteousness does not come by the law. (Gal.3:21)
2. Die to the law (ceremonial & sacrificial law), as Apostle Paul did. (Gal.2:19)	So that you might live for God. (Gal.2:19)

Pause & Think!

- *"Do we then make void the law?"* What does apostle Paul mean by this?

  Apostle Paul states, "Do we then make void the law through faith? *Certainly not! On the contrary, we establish the law."* (Rom.3:31)

- **We establish the law...**Salvation in Christ does not mean that the law has no value. In fact, justification by faith upholds the law.

- Scripture says, *Without shedding of blood there is no remission of sins.* (Heb.9:22)

In the Old Testament, animal's blood was shed for the remission of people's sins. But when Jesus died on the Cross, the blood sacrifice was made once for all as atonement for our sins.

Since Christ has fulfilled the sacrificial and the ceremonial laws at the cross, when we make peace with God through the precious blood of Jesus Christ, we establish the law. (Heb.10:10; Rom.5:1)

8.4. Righteousness, Not By The Works Of The Law

- If a law had been given that could impart life, then righteousness would certainly have come by the law. (Gal.3:21)

- A man is not justified by the works of the law but by faith in Jesus Christ; for by the works of the law (e.g. circumcision) no flesh shall be justified. (Gal.2:16)

- The Scripture declares that the whole world is a prisoner of sin. But the *righteousness from God comes through faith in Jesus Christ* to all who believe in Him. (Gal.3:22; Rom.3:22)

- Christ Jesus becomes for us wisdom from God and *righteousness and sanctification and redemption*. (1 Cor.1:30)

COMMANDMENTS OF GOD FOR US TO OBEY	REWARDS FOR OBEDIENCE/ CONSEQUENCES OF DISOBEDIENCE
Grace Of God: 1. Do not set aside the grace of God—Apostle Paul. (Gal 2.21)	i. For if righteousness comes through the law i.e., by works and not by grace, then *Christ died in vain.* (Gal.2:21) ii. For it is *by grace you have been saved*, through faith and this is not from yourselves, it is the *gift of God* not by works, so that no one can boast. (Eph.2:8-9/NIV) iii. What then? Shall we sin because we are not under law but under grace? *Certainly not!* (Rom.6:15-18)
2. Know that a person is not justified by the works of the law.—Apostle Paul. (Gal.2:16/ NIV)	But a person is *justified only by faith in Jesus Christ.*—Apostle Paul. (Gal.2:16)
3. Put your faith in Christ Jesus – Apostle Paul. (Gal.2:16/NIV)	i. So that you may be *justified by faith in Christ* and not by the works of the law (i.e. circumcision). (Gal.2:16/NIV) ii. Because by the works of the law no one will be justified. (Gal.2:16/NIV)

8.5. You Are Not Made Perfect By The Works Of The Law

COMMANDMENTS OF GOD FOR US TO OBEY	CONSEQUENCES OF DISOBEDIENCE/ SUPPORTING SCRIPTURES
To the Backslider: 1. Do not try to be made perfect by the flesh, if you have begun in the Spirit.—Apostle Paul. (Gal. 3:3; Heb.7:19) 2. Receive the Spirit by the hearing of faith and not by the works of the law.—Apostle Paul. (Gal. 3:2,5)	i. Or else, you are foolish! ii. You will suffer much for nothing.—Apostle Paul. (Gal. 3:3-4/NIV) iii. For Christ supplies the Spirit to you and works miracles among you, by the hearing of faith and not by the works of the law. (Gal.3:5)
3. Do not let anyone bewitch you from obeying the truth (concerning circumcision).—Apostle Paul. (Gal. 3:1)	i. If you do, then you are *foolish,* as apostle Paul says. ii. For before your very eyes *Jesus Christ was clearly portrayed as crucified.* (Gal. 3:1/NIV)

Pause & Think!

- After beginning your walk with the Lord in the Holy Spirit, *if you think you can be made perfect by observing the works of the law (e.g., circumcision), then you are foolish* and you will suffer much for nothing, as Apostle Paul said. (Gal.3:1-4)

- The Lord says to the backsliding believer, "Remember from where you have fallen; repent and do the first works." (Rev. 2:5)

8.6. The Holy Spirit Makes You Perfect

- *Holy Spirit through Christ, not by works of the law...*We receive the power and the anointing of the Holy Spirit only by believing in Jesus Christ, the Son of God, and not by observing the works of the law. *The Holy Spirit of God makes you perfect in the sight of God.* (Rom.8:2)

- When we rely on the power of the Holy Spirit, He enables us to resist the power of sin. For the *law of the Spirit of life in Christ Jesus sets us free from the law of sin* and death. (Rom.8:2)

- *Works of the law...*Circumcision, sacrificing animals as sin offering, following traditions, rituals, superstitions, etc., are some examples of the works of the law.

* *Since 1992, I started spending 3 to 4 hours every day praying in the Spirit and listening to the Word of God. This daily practice takes me quickly into the inner court from the outer court.*

*Then when the Lord wakes me up at 3 a.m., since I am already in the Most Holy place, His awesome Presence, **His precious Holy Spirit, like a ball of fire cleanses the temple of my spirit every day.** It is an ongoing process and Jesus still cleanses me and empowers me for His ministry and schedules each day, early in the morning itself.*

The infilling of the Holy Spirit of God helps me to die to self and to depend on the Lord rather than my own abilities.

The same anointing which I experience every day is available to you too, if you put these steps stated above, into practice. – Author

8.7. Sacrificial Law & Grace Cannot Co-Exist

- Apostle Paul states that the law is insufficient to redeem us apart from grace of Jesus Christ. (Rom.5:21; Gal.3:21)

- What the law could not do, in that it was weak through the flesh, God did by sending His own Son in the likeness of sinful flesh to be a sin offering. (Rom. 8:3)

- Jesus, by the ransom of His own blood, has redeemed us from the power of sin and therefore sin shall no longer be your master. (Rom. 6:14/NIV; 8:2)

- In fact, the name *"Jesus" means He will save His people from their sins.* (Jn. 8:36; Matt.1:21)

COMMANDMENTS OF GOD FOR US TO OBEY	CONSEQUENCES OF DISOBEDIENCE/ SUPPORTING SCRIPTURES
Abraham had two sons; one by the slave woman and the other by the free woman;	For the son of the slave woman shall **not be heir** with the son of the free woman. (Gal.4:30)
Get rid of the slave woman and her son. (Sacrificial law) (Gal.4:22,30)	(Similarly, ceremonial, sacrificial law and grace of Christ cannot co-exist.) (Gal.4:21-31)

Pause & Think!

*Get rid of the sacrificial law...*We, believers, are not children of the slave woman but of the free, i.e. we do not come under the sacrificial law but under grace of Christ. (Gal.4:31)

*Jesus Christ, our Sacrificial Lamb...*We don't need to offer animal sacrifices any more as atonement for our sins. For Christ, the Lamb of God, has been slain once for all to redeem us from our sins. (Heb.10:4; Jn.1:29; Eph.1:7)

8.8. Two Covenants—Law & Grace

- **Two sons—Slave and Free**...It is written that Abraham had two sons; one by the slave woman and the other by the free woman. (Gal.4:22)

- **Sons of Flesh and Promise**... Abraham's son by the slave woman was born according to the flesh; but his son by the free woman was born as the result of a promise of God. (Gal.4:23)

- **Two Covenants**...These things are symbolic. For **the women** *represent two covenants*. (Gal.4:24)

- **First Covenant - Hagar, the slave woman**...One covenant is from Mount Sinai and bears children who are to be slaves; this is Hagar. (Gal.4:24)

- **Hagar, the earthly Jerusalem**...Now Hagar stands for Mount Sinai in Arabia and corresponds to the present *city of Jerusalem,* because she is **in sin of slavery** with her children. (Gal.4:25)

- **Second Covenant—Sarah, The Free Woman**...But the Free woman is symbolic of the city of New Jerusalem in Heaven. (Gal.4:26)

- **Sarah, The Free Woman, The New Jerusalem**...The Free woman is symbolic of the city of New Jerusalem in Heaven. (Gal.4:26)

- **Believers, The Children of Promise**...Now we, brethren, as Isaac *was,* are children of promise. (Gal.5:28)

So then, we, believers, are not children of the slave woman but of the free woman, meaning, we no longer come under the ceremonial and sacrificial law but under the grace of Jesus Christ. (Gal.4:21-31)

8.9. Freedom In Christ

- *Freedom Through Christ…*If the Son makes you free, you shall be free indeed. It is *for freedom* that Christ has set us free. (Jn.8:36; Gal.5:1/NIV)

- *Freedom Through The Word of God…*You shall know the truth, and the truth shall make you free. (Jn.8:32)

- *Freedom Through The Holy Spirit…*The Lord is the Spirit; and where the Spirit of the Lord is, there is liberty. For the anointing breaks the yoke of bondage. (2 Cor. 3:17-18; Is.10:27)

COMMANDMENTS OF GOD	CONSEQUENCES OF DISOBEDIENCE
1. Stand fast in the liberty by which Christ has made us free. (Gal.5:1)	Apostle Paul declares that you should be *liberated from the practice of circumcision* which comes under the law.
2. Be not entangled again with a yoke of bondage. (e.g., circumcision). (Gal.5:1)	i. If you let yourselves be circumcised, then *Christ will be of no value to you at all.* (Gal.5:2/NIV)
3. Do not be circumcised.—Apostle Paul (Gal.5:2)	ii. Every man who lets himself be circumcised is *obligated to obey the whole law.* (Gal.5:3/NIV)
4. Do not let anyone hinder you from obeying the truth (concerning circumcision).—Apostle Paul. (Gal. 5:7)	iii. You who are trying to be justified by the law have been *alienated from Christ*; you have *fallen away from grace.* (Gal.5:4/NIV)
	iv. This persuasion (to do circumcision) *does not come from Him* who calls you. (Gal. 5:8)
	v. He who troubles you (in regards to circumcision), *shall bear his judgment*, whoever he is. (Gal.5:10)

COMMANDMENT OF GOD	REWARDS FOR OBEDIENCE
5. Through the Spirit, eagerly wait for the hope of *righteousness by faith* (not by the works of the law e.g., circumcision). (Gal.5:5)	i. For in Christ Jesus, neither circumcision nor uncircumcision avails anything, *but faith* working through love. (Gal.5:6/NIV) ii. In Christ Jesus, neither circumcision nor uncircumcision means anything; *what counts is a new creation.* (Gal. 6:15/NIV)

- Here, Apostle Paul was referring to the freedom, especially from the tradition of circumcision, since Christ has made us free.

- *The righteousness of God* comes only by faith in Jesus Christ through the Holy Spirit and not by circumcision, which is the work of the law. (Rom.3:22; Gal.5:5-6/NIV)

8.10. Do Not Abuse Your Freedom In Christ But Love One Another

COMMANDMENTS OF GOD FOR US TO OBEY	CONSEQUENCES OF DISOBEDIENCE/ SUPPORTING SCRIPTURES
1. *Do not use your freedom* to indulge in the sinful nature; *rather serve one another* in love. (Gal.5:13/NIV)	For you, my brothers and sisters, are *called to be free.* (Gal.5:13/NIV)
2. Love your neighbor as yourself. (Gal.5:14/NIV)	For the entire law is summed up in a single command: "Love your neighbor as yourself." (Gal.5:14/NIV)
3. Do not bite and devour each other. (Gal.5:15/NIV)	Watch out *or you will be destroyed by each other.* (Gal.5:15/NIV)

8.11. Be Led By The Holy Spirit & Not Be Under The Law

COMMANDMENTS OF GOD FOR US TO OBEY	REWARDS FOR OBEDIENCE/ CONSEQUENCES OF DISOBEDIENCE
1. Walk by the Spirit. (Gal.5:16/NIV) 2. If we live by the Spirit, let us keep in step with the Spirit. (Gal.5:25)	i. Then you will **not gratify the desires of the flesh.** (Gal.5:16/NIV) ii. For the **flesh lusts against the Spirit,** and the Spirit against the flesh; and these are contrary to one another, so that you do not do the things that you wish. (Gal.5:17) iii. If you live according to the flesh **you will die.** (Rom.8:13) iv. But if by the Spirit, you put to death the deeds of the body, **you will live.** (Rom.8:13)
3. **Be led by the Spirit.** (Gal.5:18/NIV)	i. **Then you are not under the law.** (Gal.5:18/NIV) ii. For as many as are led by the Spirit of God, these are **sons of God.** (Rom.8:14) iii. **The "Fruit of the Spirit" is:** • Love, Joy, Peace • Patience, Kindness, Goodness • Faithfulness, Gentleness • Self-Control **Against such there is no law.** (Gal.5:22-23)

8.12. The Lord Jesus Is The Spirit
(2 Cor.3:17)

Jesus Promises You Another Helper, The Holy Spirit,
For Your Victorious Life on Earth (Rom.8:1-2)

I. Who sends the Holy Spirit?

Jesus Himself sends the Holy Spirit, your Helper... Jesus stated, "I tell you the truth. It is to your advantage that I go away; for if I do not go away, *the Helper* will not come to you; but *if I depart, I will send Him to you."* (Jn.16:7)

II. Where does the Holy Spirit dwell?

*The Holy Spirit abides with you forever...*Jesus said, "The *Spirit of truth,* your helper, whom the world cannot receive, because it neither sees Him nor knows Him; but *you know Him,* for *He dwells with you and will be in you."* (Jn.14:16-17)

III. What does the Holy Spirit do for you?

- *The Holy Spirit helps you obey the Lord's Commandments...*Jesus said, "If you love Me, keep My commandments. And I will pray the Father, and He will give you *another Helper,* that He may abide with you forever." (Jn.14:15-16)

- *The Holy Spirit teaches and reminds you of all of Jesus' Words...*Jesus declared, "The Helper, the Holy Spirit, whom the Father will send in My name, *He will teach you all things,* and bring to your remembrance all things that I said to you." (Jn.14:25-26)

- *The Holy Spirit convicts the world of sin, of righteousness, and judgment...*Jesus explained, "The Spirit of truth will convict the world of sin, and of righteousness, and of judgment:

    i. of sin, because they do not believe in Me;

ii. of righteousness, because I go to My Father and you see Me no more;

iii. of judgment, because the ruler of this world, Satan, is judged." (Jn.16:8-11)

iv. **Repent and be baptized** in the name of Jesus Christ for the forgiveness of your sins. And **you will receive the gift of the Holy Spirit.** (Acts 2:38)

- **The Spirit of Truth guides you into all truth...**

  i. Jesus stated, "The Holy Spirit will not speak on His own authority,

  ii. but **whatever He hears He will speak**; and

  iii. He will tell you things to come.

  iv. **He will glorify Me**,

  v. for He will take of what is Mine and declare it to you." (Jn.16:13-15)

- **The Holy Spirit gives you liberty...**Now the Lord is the Spirit; and where the Spirit of the Lord *is*, there *is* liberty. (2 Cor.3:17)

- **The Holy Spirit empowers you...** Jesus assured, "You shall **receive power** when the Holy Spirit comes upon you." (Acts1:4-8)

- **The Holy Spirit helps you bear witness for Christ...**Jesus assured, "When the Helper comes, whom I shall send to you from the Father, the Spirit of truth who proceeds from the Father, He will testify of Me. And you also will bear witness." (Jn.15:26-27)

- **The Holy Spirit makes you witnesses of Jesus to all nations...** Jesus declared, "You shall be witnesses to Me in Jerusalem, and in all Judea and Samaria, and **to the end of the earth.**" (Acts 1:4-8)

IV. *When did Jesus breathe the Holy Spirit on His disciples?*

*Jesus equips His disciples for their Mission...*Jesus said to His disciples, "Peace to you! As the Father has sent Me, *I also send you.*"

And when He had said this, He breathed on them, and said to them, *"Receive the Holy Spirit."* (Jn.20:21-22)

Receive the Power of The Holy Spirit

V. How do you receive the Holy Spirit?

Steps to follow... Ask, Wait, Tarry and Be Baptized with the Holy Spirit.

- **Ask**...Jesus declared, "I say to you, ask, and it will be given to you; seek, and you will find; knock, and it will be opened to you.

- If a son asks for bread from any father among you, will he give him a stone? Or if *he asks* for a fish, will he give him a serpent instead of a fish? Or if he asks for an egg, will he offer him a scorpion?

  If *you then, being evil*, know how to give good gifts to your children, *how much more will your heavenly Father give the Holy Spirit to those who ask Him*!" (Lk.11:9-13)

- *Wait for the promise, the Holy Spirit*...Jesus, being assembled together with the disciples, commanded them not to depart from Jerusalem, but to *wait for the Promise of the Father*, which," He said, "you have heard from Me." (Acts 1:4-8)

- *Tarry until you are endued with the power of the Holy Spirit*...Jesus commanded His disciples, "Behold, I send the Promise of My Father upon you; but *tarry* in the city of Jerusalem until you are endued with power from on high." (Lk.24:49)

- *Be baptized with the Holy Spirit*... Jesus declared, "For John truly baptized with water, but *you shall be baptized with the Holy Spirit* not many days from now." (Acts 1:5)

VI. Which fruit of the Holy Spirit will manifest through you?

- *The Holy Spirit gives you the fruit of the Spirit*... The fruit of the Spirit is love, joy, peace, longsuffering, kindness, goodness, faithfulness, gentleness, self-control. (Gal.5:22-23)

- *The Holy Spirit pours God's Love in your heart*...God's love is poured out into our hearts through the Holy Spirit, who has been given to us. (Rom.5:5)

- *The Holy Spirit intercedes with divine love for the lost souls*... We do not know what we should pray for as we ought, but the *Spirit Himself makes intercession for us* and for the salvation of the lost souls with groanings which cannot be uttered. (Rom.8:26)

- The Spirit of God makes intercession through you *for the saints according to the will of God.* (Rom.8:27)

VII. *Why do you need the Holy Spirit in your life?*

- *The Holy Spirit delivers you from Condemnation of sin...* There is no condemnation to those who are in Christ Jesus, who *do not walk according to the flesh, but according to the Spirit.* (Rom.8:1)

- *The Holy Spirit helps you lead a Victorious Life on earth...*For the law of the Spirit of life in Christ Jesus has made me *free from the law of sin and death.* The more of the Holy Spirit you have, the more you will be dead to sin. (Rom.8:2)

- *The Holy Spirit makes you an overcomer...*The Holy Spirit helps you in your weaknesses to overcome the lust of the eyes, lust of the flesh and the pride of life. (Rom. 8:26; 1 Jn.2:15-17)

- *The Holy Spirit guarantees your inheritance in Heaven...* In Christ, you are sealed with the Holy Spirit of promise, who is the *guarantee of your inheritance until the redemption* of the purchased possession (a believer). (Eph.1:13-14; 2 Cor.5:5)

VIII. *To whom does the Lord give the Holy Spirit?*

- *"I will pour out My Spirit on all flesh* before the coming of the great and awesome day of the LORD," declares the Lord God Almighty. You can claim this promise of the Lord for yourself and for your children since we are living in the last days. (Joel 2:28, 31)

- *Believe in Christ and be sealed with the Holy Spirit of God...*When you hear the Word of Truth, the Gospel of your Salvation and believe in Christ, you are sealed with the Holy Spirit of promise. (Eph.1:13)

IX. *What increases the Anointing of the Holy Spirit on you?*

- *Prayer brings down the Holy Spirit...*

  When you spend time in prayer, the Holy Spirit of God fills your spirit and you feel satisfied in your heart.

  In the Acts of the Apostles when the disciples prayed, *the place where they were assembled together was shaken*; and they were all *filled with the Holy Spirit,* and they spoke the Word of God with boldness. (Acts 1:12-2:4; 4:31)

- *Praying in the Spirit uplifts you...* When you pray in the Spirit, the anointing of the Holy Spirit increases upon you and edifies you. For the Scripture says that he who speaks in a tongue *edifies himself.* (1 Cor.14:4; Acts 2:1-4)

- *Thirst & Wait on the Lord to receive the rivers of Living Water...*

  Jesus said, "If anyone *thirsts,* let him come to Me and drink. He who believes in Me, out of his heart will flow *rivers of Living Water."* (Jn.7:37-38)

  The glory of God fills your heart when you wait on the Lord in the Most Holy Place early in the morning, preferably between 3-6 am, when your mind is at rest.

- *God's Word Increases the Anointing...*

  Meditating the Word of God will increase the anointing on you and you will feel uplifted in your spirit. You will also experience the joy of the Holy Spirit in your heart.

  In the Acts of the Apostles, when the people *heard Peter preaching the Word of God,* they were cut to the heart and then Peter said to them, *"Repent,* and let every one of you be baptized in the name of Jesus Christ for the remission of sins; and you shall *receive the gift of the Holy Spirit.* (Ps.19:7-11; Eph.1:13; Acts 2:14-38)

- *Obeying the call of God releases God's Power...*

  When you have a specific calling, as you yield, the Lord equips you with the power of the Holy Spirit to fulfill the call of God on your life.

For example, Peter was called to be a fisher of men. After receiving the power of the Holy Spirit at Pentecost, Peter preached the Word with boldness and three thousand people were saved in one day. (Acts.2:41)

Similarly, from the Scriptures we know that people of God like *Moses, David, Samson, Prophet Ezekiel, John the Baptist, Peter, John, Philip, Apostle Paul,* etc., operated in the power of God and fulfilled their mission on earth.

- *Doing the will of God releases the Anointing...*

Scripture says that God, our Savior, desires *all men to be saved,* which is His perfect will. (1 Tim.2:4)

When you please the Lord by standing in the gap and agonizing for lost souls, the Lord fills you with the rivers of Living Water and He increases the burden in your spirit to intercede for perishing souls.

- *Resisting Sin by yielding to the Holy Spirit increases the Anointing...*

As long as you are willing to resist sin, the Lord will empower you with His Holy Spirit to overcome the temptation and not to be ensnared in that sin. (2 Cor.12:9)

- *Obedience to God's Commandments increases the Anointing...*

When you obey the Commandments of God out of love for Christ, Jesus Christ Himself, along with Father God, will come and dwell in you. (Jn.14:21, 23)

- *Suffering for Christ releases the Anointing...*

When you suffer for Christ, His grace and anointing will be given to you to endure the sufferings for Him.

The Lord said to Apostle Paul, *"My grace* is sufficient for you, for *My power* is made perfect in weakness." (2 Cor.12:9)

The God of all grace, who called you to His eternal glory in Christ, after you have suffered a little while, will Himself restore you and make you strong, firm and steadfast. (1 Pet.5:10/NIV)

X. *How do you lose God's Anointing?*

You can leak out the anointing of the Holy Spirit...

- When you talk vain things and gossip about people.
- When you indulge in worldly pleasures related to sexual immorality, e.g. King David. (2 Sam.11-12, Ps.51:1-12)
- When you take part in worldly pleasures, such as, watching movies, TV serials, etc. (Jas.4:4; Rom.8:7-8)
- When you willfully sin and rebel against God, e.g., King Saul (1 Sam. 13, 15)
- When you deliberately disobey God's Commandments, e.g., Samson, King Saul, etc. (Judg.14-16; 1 Sam.16:14)

*Depression & Sadness will overtake you...*When you leak out the Holy Spirit by persisting in sin, you feel empty inside. Depression and sadness fill your heart. This is the reason why, when King David committed the sin of adultery, he cried out to God to restore unto him the *joy of God's salvation* and to *uphold him with His generous Spirit.* (Ps.51:10-12)

PART II

Commandments Of God From
The Book Of Ephesians

Book of Ephesians

Apostle Paul, a faithful servant of Jesus Christ, addressed this epistle to the Saints at Ephesus in Asia Minor. He wrote this letter in the year 62 A.D., most likely in Rome, where he was a prisoner for his faith in Christ.

*The **Two Main Themes** of this Letter...*

* Redemption in Christ.
* New Life in Christ.

Purpose:

Paul's main purpose for writing Ephesians is given in Chapter 1:15-17. Here, Apostle Paul prayerfully longs for believers in Christ to advance in *faith, love, wisdom and revelation* of the Father of glory. Paul earnestly desires that believers grow in Christian character and live life worthy of Christ. (Eph.4:1-3; 5:1-2)

In this epistle, Apostle Paul also emphasizes the *role of the Holy Spirit* in the Christian life. (Eph.1:13-14, 17; 2:18; 3:16; 4:3-4, 30; 5:18; 6:17-18)

*"**Put it into practice** - whatever you have learned, or received or heard from me, or seen in me,"* says Apostle Paul. (Phil.4:9)

1. Called To Live To The Praise of God's Glory

COMMANDMENT OF GOD FOR US TO OBEY	REWARDS FOR OBEDIENCE/ SUPPORTING SCRIPTURES
1. *You, who trust in Christ, should live to the praise* of His Glory. - Apostle Paul (Eph.1:12)	*Why should we live to the praise of God's glory?* 1. For God has *blessed us* in the heavenly realms *with every spiritual blessing* in Christ. (Eph.1:3/NIV) 2. For God *chose us* in Christ *before the creation of the world to be holy* and blameless in His sight. (Eph.1:4/NIV) 3. In love, God *predestined us* to be *adopted as His sons* through Jesus Christ, in accordance *with His pleasure* and *will.* (Eph.1:5/NIV) 4. God *predestined us* and adopted us as His sons **to the praise of His glorious grace.** (Eph.1:6/NIV) 5. God has *freely given us His glorious grace* in the One He loves, Jesus Christ. (Eph.1:6/NIV) 6. In Christ, we have *redemption through His blood.* (Eph.1:7/NIV) 7. In Christ, we have the *forgiveness of sins,* in accordance with the *riches of God's grace* that He *lavished on us* with all wisdom and understanding (knowing our rebellious nature). (Eph.1:8/NIV)

COMMANDMENT OF GOD	REWARDS FOR OBEDIENCE/ SUPPORTING SCRIPTURES
1. *You, who trust in Christ, should live to the praise* of His Glory. - Apostle Paul (Eph.1:12)	8. God *made known to us the mystery of His will according to His good pleasure* which He purposed in Christ. (Eph.1:9/NIV)
	9. God made known to us the *mystery of His will* to be put into effect when the times reach their fulfillment—*to bring all things* in heaven and on earth together *under one head, even Christ Jesus.* (Eph.1:10/NIV)
	10. In Christ, we have *obtained an inheritance*, being predestined *according to the purpose of God* who works all things according to the counsel of His will. (Eph.1:11)
	Praise be to the God and Father of our Lord Jesus Christ who has blessed us with all the above spiritual blessings in Christ. (Eph.1:3/NIV)
2. Hear the Word of Truth, the gospel of your salvation. – Apostle Paul (Eph.1:13)	Then you will trust in Christ. - Apostle Paul (Eph.1:13)

1.1. How Can We Live To The Praise Of God's Glory?

Holy Spirit, the Guarantee of Your Inheritance In Heaven... We can live to the praise of God's glory only by the power of the Holy Spirit.

COMMANDMENTS OF GOD FOR US TO OBEY	REWARDS FOR OBEDIENCE/ SUPPORTING SCRIPTURES
1. Believe in Christ. - Apostle Paul (Eph.1:12-13/NIV)	i. *When you believe in Christ...*You are *sealed with the Holy Spirit* of promise, who is the *guarantee* of your inheritance until the redemption of the purchased possession, *to the praise of His glory.* (Eph.1:14) ii. The Spirit also *helps in our weaknesses.* (Rom.8:26) iii For we do not know what we should pray for as we ought, but the *Spirit Himself makes intercession for us* with groaning which cannot be uttered. (Rom.8:26) iv. Now He who searches the hearts knows what the mind of the Spirit *is,* because He *makes intercession for the saints according to the will of God.* (Rom.8:26-27)
You are created in Christ for good works... 2. Do good works, which God prepared in advance for us to do. (Eph.2:10/NIV)	i. For you are God's workmanship, created in Christ Jesus to do good works. (Eph.2:10) ii. Let your light so shine before men, that *they may see your good works, and glorify your Father* who is in heaven. (Matt.5:16/KJV)

Pause & Think!

- The Holy Spirit not only guarantees your inheritance in heaven but also helps you to overcome *your weaknesses on earth,* thereby enabling you to live to the praise of His glory. (Eph.1:14; Rom.8:26-27)

- After you believe in Christ and accept Him as your Lord and Savior, only then the good works which you do on earth will be credited to your account for your rewards in Heaven.

- *Every good work that you do after your Salvation counts* and is written in the books in Heaven (Books of Good and Evil) and you will be rewarded accordingly on the day of Judgment. (Eccl. 12:14; 2 Cor.5:10; Rev.20:12)

Is The Holy Spirit A Real Person?

- The Holy Spirit is one of the three persons in the Holy Trinity and He is the One who is on the earth today, after Christ ascended to Heaven. (Jn.14:17)

- The Holy Spirit is a very gentle Spirit who can be easily grieved. (Eph.4:30)

- The Holy Spirit of God is a real person. He has feelings, emotions, intellect and willpower of His own. (1 Cor.12:11)

- The Holy Spirit thinks, loves, gives, receives, perceives and also *communicates* like us. He loves to have fellowship with us more than we desire to be with Him.

- *The Holy Spirit imparts gifts* and talents to the children of God according to His will. (1 Cor.12:11)

- *The Holy Spirit gives us power* to live a victorious Christian life. (Gal.5:16)

- The Holy Spirit is as powerful as Father God and Jesus Christ but He functions differently. (1 Jn.5:7; Jn.14:26; 15:26)

- *Be Warned:* We, believers in Christ, have the power to stop the Holy Spirit – by grieving, resisting & quenching the Spirit of God. (Eph.4:30; Acts 7:51; 1 Thess.5:19)

1.2. The Exceeding Greatness Of God's Power Available To Believers In Christ

I. The incomparable great power of the Holy Spirit that is available to us, believers, is like the working of *God's mighty power, which He exerted in Christ...*

    i. when God raised Christ from the dead;

    ii. when God seated Christ at His right hand in the heavenly realms,

    iii. *far above all rule, and authority, and power, and dominion, and*

    iv. *far above every name that is named,*

    v. not only in this world, but also in that which is to come; and

    vi. *God has put all things under Christ's feet;* and

    vii. God appointed *Christ to be Head* over everything for the church, which is His body.

    viii. The *fullness of Christ fills all in all.* (Eph.1:19-23)

II. *You Too Can Receive His Awesome Power...*Can you imagine that this awesome power of the Holy Spirit that worked in Christ Jesus is also available to us, the faithful believers?

Jesus exhorts us to *keep on asking, seeking and knocking* at Heaven's door *until we receive the fullness of the Holy Spirit;* for Jesus Himself prayed fervently and received the *Holy Spirit without measure.* (Matt.7:7; Jn.3:34; Lk.3:21-22; 11:9-13)

As a believer, if you are still in bondage and have not overcome sin, Satan and the world, as Jesus did, it means that *you are not using the fullness of the power of the Holy Spirit* that is available to you. How sad!

Do Not Let Satan Speak to Your Mind

2. How Not To Live In The Futility Of The Mind

*Spirit, Soul & Body...*We, human beings, are made up of spirit, soul (mind) and body. Scientists say that our spirit which is lodged in between our rib cage weighs about 21 grams. (1 Thes.5:23)

*Spirit saved at Salvation...*When we accept Christ as our Savior, only our spirit is saved and it is saved forever, unless otherwise we rebel against God and choose to lose our Salvation, like Judas did. (2 Cor.5:17; Eph.2:4-5)

*Soul being saved life long...*Our soul, which deals with our feelings, emotions, thought life, intelligence and will power, is being saved throughout our life. (Jas.1:21; 1Pet.1:8-9)

Body saved at Resurrection... Once our spirit is saved, we should **guard our Salvation with fear and trembling** all our life **by obeying the commandments of God**, then our body will be saved in the resurrection, when we put on immortality. (Phil.2:12; 1 Cor.15:42-55)

*Watch out! Satan influences our Mind through our five senses...*If we are not careful and if we allow our mind to be corrupted with the filth of this world, then heed the warning of the Lord. He **warns us by saying, "Why should you be beaten anymore? Your whole head is sick,** and your whole heart is afflicted. From the top of your head to the soles of your feet, there is no soundness, but wounds and bruises and putrefying sores; they have not been closed or bound up, or **soothed with healing ointment of God's Word."** (Is.1:5-6; Prov.3:8)

*Repent or else the Lord will not hear your Prayers...*If we don't repent, change our ways and fill our minds with the pure, holy and righteous thoughts, then the Lord says to us, "When you spread out your hands, I will hide My eyes from you; even though **you make many prayers, I will not hear."** (Is. 1:15; Phil.4:8)

Heed the Warning of the Lord today..."Wash yourselves, make yourselves clean. **If you are willing and obedient, you shall eat the good of the land;** but if you refuse and *rebel, you shall be devoured by the sword,*" for the mouth of the Lord has spoken this. (Is.1:16, 19-20)

*Either be hot or cold but not lukewarm...*If we continue to fill our mind with vain, unrighteous, impure, immoral or lustful thoughts, eventually *we will leak out the Anointing of the Holy Spirit* and we will become neither hot nor cold but lukewarm and the Lord says that *He will spit us out of His mouth.* So let us heed the warning of the Lord today. (Rev.3:15-16)

❖ *To be Carnally Minded is Enmity Against God...*

You can keep yourself occupied with the following:

o   Get involved in a Sports activity.

o   Learn to play a musical instrument.

o   Develop productive, non-sinful hobbies.

o   Read inspiring biographies of "Pioneers of Faith" (E.g. D.L.Moody, George Muller, Rees Howells, John Wesley, etc.) which will help your spirit man to grow.

o   Watch Biblical movies.

o   Listen to audio Bible.

o   Watch History Channel, National Geography Channel on TV.

o   Watch Wild Life Channels like Animal Kingdom.

o   Watch Sports Channels.

o   Attend Christian or Classical Music Concerts.

o   Do Painting, Digital Arts, Animation, etc.

o   Participate in Church Activities.

o   Listen to Christian Worship Music.

2.1. Put Off Your Former Way Of Life

COMMANDMENTS OF GOD	CONSEQUENCES OF DISOBEDIENCE
1. You, no longer live *as the Gentiles do*, in the futility of their *thinking.* (Eph.4:17/NIV)	i. For the Gentiles (unbelievers) are *darkened* in their *understanding.* (Eph.4:18/NIV)
2. You, put off your former way of life, your old self, which is being corrupted by its deceitful desires. (Eph.4:22/NIV)	ii. *They are separated from the Life of God* because of the *ignorance* that is in them due to the *hardening of their hearts.* (Eph.4:18/NIV)
	iii. Having *lost all sensitivity*, they have given themselves over to *sensuality,* so as to indulge in every kind of *impurity*, with the *continual lust* for more. (Eph.4:19/NIV)
	iv. However, this is not the way of life you (believers) learned when you heard about Christ and were taught in Him in accordance with the truth that is in Jesus. (Eph.4:20-21/NIV)
3. *Do not follow the ways of this world,* and of the ruler of the kingdom of the air, *the evil spirit* who is now at work in those who are *disobedient*. (Eph.2:2/NIV)	Or else, you will *die in your transgressions* and sins. (Eph.2:1-2/NIV)

❖ **Avoid Bad Friends:** When friends entice you to...

o   smoke cigarettes,
o   drink alcohol,
o   watch filthy movies,
o   commit sexually immoral acts,
o   do drugs,
o   gamble, etc.

Then it indicates that they are of the world. Therefore stay away from them and avoid their path. Cling to Jesus and **make Jesus your Best Friend!** (Prov.4:14-15; Ps.1:1-3)

2.2. When You Defile Your Mind You Offer Defiled Sacrifice To The Lord

o *"Do Not Offer Defiled Sacrifice On My Altar,"* says the Lord of Hosts. (Mal.1:7-8)

o Brethren, you *present your bodies a living sacrifice,* holy, acceptable unto God. (Rom.12:1)

I. *Walk Worthy of Your Calling*

• When you want to please God at any cost and desire to fulfill His will for your life, then you should be very careful with your walk with the Lord.

• *Do not rebel against God...*If you don't guard your heart and harbor even a little disappointment against the Lord, you will tend to rebel against Him. Immediately, Satan, the deceiver, will try to *distract you with the things of the world.* (2 Cor.11:3).

II. *How Do You Defile Your Mind?*

i. Satan attacks your mind:

If the devil cannot make you fall into big temptations, he will divert you by attacking your mind in a subtle way. You should be careful what you fill your mind with; *for as a man thinks, so shall he be.* (Prov.23:7)

Do not corrupt your mind by watching filthy, lustful, perverse or sexually immoral scenes from movies, TV, internet, cell phones, etc., which *affect your sensuality and emotions.* This is sinful in the eyes of God. Even though it may seem to be a light entertainment to you, it defiles your mind. And the *carnal mind is enmity against God.* (Rom.8:7)

ii. You are the temple of the Holy Spirit:

Since Christ is enthroned in your heart, do you think the Lord can watch those sensual scenes with you? The Lord says, *Do not offer defiled sacrifice on My altar.* Is it not evil? *Offer it to your governor!* Would he be pleased with you? (Mal.1:7-9)

III. *You May Lose God's Favor*

When you offer defiled sacrifice, i.e. your corrupted mind to the Lord, and then you entreat God's favor, He may not be gracious to you. He will not accept you favorably. (Mal.1:7-9)

IV. *Consequences, If You Do Not Renew Your Mind*

If you ignore the repeated convictions of the Holy Spirit and persist in the futility of your thinking, then you will face the following consequences:

1. You will be *darkened* in your *understanding.*
2. You will be *separated from the Life of God* and become dead in your spirit by leaking out the Holy Spirit from within you.
3. You will be *ignorant of God's ways and lose God's blessings.*
4. Your *heart will become hardened.*
5. You will *lose all sensitivity to the Holy Spirit.*
6. You will give yourself over to *sensuality,* so as to indulge in every kind of *impurity,* with the *continual lust* for more. (Eph.4:18-19; 1 Cor.7:5)

V. *Sanctify Your Mind*

- *The Word of God renews your mind:* Therefore, be transformed by renewing your mind constantly with the pure Word of God. (Rom.12:2; Jn.17:17)
- *The Holy Spirit governs your mind:* The mind governed by the Spirit is life and peace but the mind governed by the flesh is death. (Rom.8:6)

2.3. Be Renewed In The Spirit Of Your Mind

COMMANDMENTS OF GOD FOR US TO OBEY	REWARDS FOR OBEDIENCE/ SUPPORTING SCRIPTURES
1. Be renewed in the spirit of your mind. (Eph. 4:23) 2. You, **put on the new self,** created to be like God, in true righteousness and holiness. —Apostle Paul. (Eph. 4:24/NIV) 3. Do not conform any longer to the pattern of this world; but be transformed by the **renewing of your mind (with the Word of God).** —Apostle Paul. (Rom.12:2; Phil.4:8/NIV)	For you, believers, were taught in accordance with **the truth that is in Jesus.** So be made new in the **attitude** of your minds. —Apostle Paul. (Eph. 4:21-23/NIV)

Some of the ways you can renew your mind...

- *Think on true and pure things...*

    Finally, brethren,

    whatsoever things are **true,**

    whatsoever things are **honest,**

    whatsoever things are **just,**

    whatsoever things are **pure,**

    whatsoever things are **lovely,**

    whatsoever things are of **good report;**

    if there be any virtue, and if there be any praise, **think on these things.** (Phil.4:8/KJV)

- *Meditate on God's Word day and night...*Scripture also says, delight in the law of the Lord and meditate on His Word day and night. For God's Word is true, honest, just, pure, lovely and of good report. (Ps.1:2; 119)

- *100% Obedience to God's Word...*We should not only meditate God's Word day and night but we also need to be doers of God's Word – Not 10% or 40% or 80% but 100%. This should be our ultimate goal to achieve, in order to keep our soul (mind) and body holy before God.

How can we be Doers of God's Word?

We can be doers of God's Word...

o   by walking in *total submission to God,*

o   by relying on the power of the Holy Spirit,

o   when we desire to please the Lord at any cost,

o   when we have *reverential fear of God,*

o   when we truly love Jesus,

o   when we don't want to grieve the Holy Spirit,

o   when we deny ourselves and crucify our flesh on the cross,

o   when we fear *God's chastisement* and discipline for our disobedience.

The Lord let the Israelites die while wandering in the desert for 40 years because of their disobedience and rebellion. Ask God to fill you with the *"Spirit of Obedience."* (Num.14; Rom.8:13)

- *Bring every wrong thought captive to the obedience of Christ...*We demolish arguments and every pretension that sets itself up against the knowledge of God, and we take captive every thought to make it obedient to Christ. (2 Cor.10:5/NIV)

2.4. How To Put On The New Self

(Fruits of New Self)

If anyone is in Christ, he is a new creation; old things have passed away; behold, all things have become new. (2 Cor. 5:17)

When you obey the following commandments, the fruits of the new self will manifest in your life.

COMMANDMENTS OF GOD FOR US TO OBEY	REWARDS FOR OBEDIENCE/ CONSEQUENCES OF DISOBEDIENCE
Truthfulness: 1. Put away lying, and let each one of you speak truth with his neighbor. (Eph. 4:25)	For we are all members of one body (Body of Christ). (Eph.4:25/NIV)
Put Away Anger: 2. (i) In your anger, do not sin. (ii) Do not let the sun go down while you are still angry. (Eph. 4:26/NIV)	Or else, you will give **place to the devil**. (Eph.4:27)
Steal No Longer: 3. Let him who stole steal no longer, but rather let him labor, working with his hands what is good. (Eph. 4:28)	So that he may have something to share with those in need. (Eph.4:28/NIV)
No Corrupt Communication: 4. Do not let any unwholesome talk come out of your mouths, but only what is helpful for building others up according to their needs. (Eph.4:29/NIV)	So that it may benefit those who listen. (Eph.4:29/NIV)
Grieve Not the Holy Spirit: 5. Do not grieve the Holy Spirit of God. (Eph.4:30)	By whom you were sealed for the day of redemption. (Eph.4:30)

COMMANDMENTS OF GOD FOR US TO OBEY	REWARDS FOR OBEDIENCE/ CONSEQUENCES OF DISOBEDIENCE
No Bitterness, Hatred, etc. 6. Get rid of all bitterness, rage and anger, brawling and slander, along with every form of malice. (Eph.4:31/NIV)	A gentle answer turns away wrath, but a harsh word stirs up anger. (Prov.15:1/NIV)
Kindness & Forgiveness: 7. Be kind and compassionate to one another, forgiving each other. (Eph.4:32/NIV)	Just as in Christ God forgave you. (Eph.4:32/NIV)
Life of Love: 8. Be imitators of God, as dearly loved children and live a life of love. (Eph.5:1-2/NIV)	Just as Christ loved us and gave Himself up for us as a fragrant offering and sacrifice to God. (Eph.5:2/NIV)
No Sexual Immorality & Greed: 9. Fornication and all uncleanness or covetousness, let it not even be named among you. (Eph.5:3)	Because these are improper for God's holy people. (Eph.5:3/NIV)
No Obscenity & Foolish Talk: 10. Let there not be obscenity, foolish talk or coarse joking, which are out of place but rather thanksgiving. (Eph.5:4/NIV)	For no immoral, impure or greedy person—such a man is an idolater—has any *inheritance in the Kingdom of Christ* and of God. (Eph.5:5/NIV)
No Deception: 11(i) Let no one deceive you with empty words. (Eph.5:6/NIV) (ii) Do not be partners with them. (Eph.5:7/NIV)	For because of such things *God's wrath* comes on those who are *disobedient*. (Eph.5:6/NIV)

*Point to Ponder…*Paul explains here that certain people might deceive you into believing that one can have an unrighteous lifestyle and still make it to Heaven which is not true. He warns us not to be partners with such people.

COMMANDMENTS OF GOD FOR US TO OBEY	REWARDS FOR OBEDIENCE/ CONSEQUENCES OF DISOBEDIENCE
Be Children of Light: 12 (i) Live as children of light. (Eph.5:8/NIV) (ii) And **find out what pleases the Lord**. (Eph.5:10/NIV)	i. For you were once darkness, but now you are light in the Lord. (Eph.5:8/NIV) ii. For the fruit of the light consists in all goodness, righteousness and truth. (Eph.5:9/NIV)
Get rid of Fruitless Deeds: 13. Have nothing to do with the fruitless deeds of darkness, but rather expose them. (Eph.5:11/NIV)	i. For **it is shameful even to mention what the disobedient do in secret.** (Eph.5:12/NIV) ii. Everything exposed by the light becomes visible. iii. For it is **light that makes everything visible**. (Eph.5:13/NIV)
Rise from the dead: 14. **Wake up, O sleeper;** rise from the dead. (Eph.5:14/NIV)	And Christ will shine on you. (Eph.5:14/NIV)
Redeem your time: 15 (i) Be very careful, how you live - not as unwise but as wise, making the most of every opportunity. (Eph.5:15-16/NIV) (ii) Redeem your time. (Eph.5:16)	**Because the days are evil.** (Eph.5:15-16)

COMMANDMENTS OF GOD FOR US TO OBEY	REWARDS FOR OBEDIENCE/ CONSEQUENCES OF DISOBEDIENCE
Discern God's Will: 16. Do not be foolish but understand what the Lord's will is. (Eph.5:17/NIV)	*Ask God to fill you with the knowledge of His will* through all spiritual wisdom and understanding; in order that you may live a life worthy of the Lord and may please Him in every way. (Col.1:9-10/NIV)
Avoid Alcoholism: 17 (i) *Do not get drunk on wine.* (Eph.5:18/NIV)	Which leads to *debauchery, i.e. wickedness.* (Eph.5:18/NIV)
(ii) *Do not look at wine* when it is red, when it sparkles in the cup and goes down smoothly. (Prov.23:29-35)	i. In the end *it bites like a serpent* and stings like an adder. ii. Your eyes will *see strange things.* iii. And your heart *utter perverse things.* (Prov.23:29-35)

2.5. Can A Christian Drink Alcohol?

I. Alcoholic Addiction:

- *Definition of alcohol:* A colorless, volatile, flammable liquid produced by the natural fermentation of sugars, the intoxicating constituent of liquors (beer, wine or whisky) that can make a person drunk.

- *Statistics in US:* A recent study shows United States has become the world's largest wine consumer. About 79 million Americans, ages 21-38 drank wine in 2015 – an average of 2 cases per person. Alcoholic addiction is a serious concern which needs to be dealt with.

- *Standard alcoholic drinks in US:* 12 ounces of regular beer that usually has about 5% alcohol and 5 ounces of wine which typically has about 12% alcohol.

- *Reasons why people resort to alcohol:* In order to drown their sorrows, pain, fears, anxiety, worries, marital discord, etc.

II. Biblical Consequences Of Drinking Wine:

1. The wise king Solomon said, *"Wine is a mocker,* strong drink a *brawler,* and whoever is led astray by it is *not wise."* (Prov.20:1)

2. *"Woe to those* who are heroes at *drinking wine,* and valiant men in mixing *strong drink."* (Is.5:22)

3. *"Who has woe?*

   Who has *sorrow?*

   Who has *strife?*

   Who has complaining?

   Who has *wounds* without cause?

   Who has redness of eyes?

   Those who tarry long over wine; those who go to try mixed wine."* (Prov.23:29-35)

4. "Woe to those *who rise early in the morning that they may run* after strong drink, *who tarry late into the evening as wine inflames them!" (Is.5:11)*

5. *Eternal Damnation for Drunkenness:* The *works of the flesh* are evident, which are: adultery, fornication, uncleanness, lewdness, idolatry, sorcery, hatred, contentions, jealousies, outbursts of wrath, selfish ambitions, dissensions, heresies, envy, murders, *drunkenness,* revelries, and the like; and those who practice such things *will not inherit the Kingdom of God.* (Gal.5:19-21)

III. Medical Consequences Of Wine On Our Body:

- *Short term negative effects of alcohol:* Distorted vision, hearing, coordination, altered perceptions and emotions, impaired judgment, bad breath, nausea, vomiting, and hangovers, etc. can occur after drinking over a relatively short period of time. Even in moderation, alcohol use causes significant problems – physically, mentally and spiritually. It is no wonder the Bible consistently warns against it.

- *Long term negative effects of alcohol:* Other problems, such as, liver disease, heart disease, high blood pressure, stroke, certain forms of cancer, and pancreatitis – often develop more gradually and may become evident only after years of drinking.

IV. Be Separated Unto Jesus!

o *A drinking servant is unprepared for His Lord's return.* (Matt.24:48-51)

o The intoxicating wine takes away one's understanding and intelligence. (Hos.4:11)

o If a Christian is a drinker, *do not associate with him.* (1 Cor.5:11)

o Jesus wants to give you an abundant life. (Jn.10:10)

V. The Holy Spirit Will Deliver You From Alcoholism:

- The Scripture says, "Do not get drunk on wine; *instead, be filled with the Holy Spirit of God;"* for He is the real joy Giver. (Eph.5:18/NIV; Rom.14:17; Jn.16:24)

- The Holy Spirit is the One who can help you overcome the addiction of alcoholism; *for the Spirit helps in your weaknesses.* (Rom.8:26)

2.6. Fruits of New Self–Be Filled With The Holy Spirit

COMMANDMENTS OF GOD FOR US TO OBEY	REWARDS FOR OBEDIENCE/ SUPPORTING SCRIPTURES
Infilling of the Holy Spirit: 18 (i) Be filled with the Spirit. (Eph.5:18/NIV) (ii) Be baptized with the Holy Spirit. (Acts 1:4-5)	i. The disciples were *all filled with the Holy Spirit and began to speak in other tongues,* as the Spirit gave them utterance. (Acts 2:1-47) ii. You will *receive power* when the Holy Spirit comes upon you and you will *be My witnesses.*—Jesus. (Acts 1:8)

Desire for the 9 Gifts of the Holy Spirit

- There are diversities of *gifts,* but the same Spirit.
- There are differences of *ministries,* but the same Lord.
- And there are diversities of *activities,* but it is the same God who works all in all.
- But the manifestation of the Spirit is given to each one *for the profit of all;*
- for to one is given the *word of wisdom* through the Spirit,
- to another the *word of knowledge* through the same Spirit,
- to another *faith* by the same Spirit,
- to another *gifts of healings* by the same Spirit,
- to another the *working of miracles,*
- to another *prophecy,*
- to another *discerning of spirits,*
- to another *different kinds of tongues,*
- to another the *interpretation of tongues.*
- But one and the same Spirit works all these things, *distributing to each one individually as He wills.* (1 Cor.12:4-11)

Wait on the Lord until you receive the Gifts of the Holy Spirit to have a powerful Ministry, to expand God's Kingdom!

2.7. Fruits of New Self–Sing Unto The Lord

COMMANDMENTS OF GOD FOR US TO OBEY	REWARDS FOR OBEDIENCE/ SUPPORTING SCRIPTURES
Spiritual Songs: 19. Speak to one another with psalms, hymns and spiritual songs. (Eph.5:19)	*Let the Word of Christ dwell in you richly as you teach and admonish one another with all wisdom,* and *as you sing psalms, hymns* and *spiritual songs* with gratitude in your hearts to God. (Col.3:16/NIV)
Sing unto the Lord: 20. (i) Sing and make music from your heart to the Lord. (ii) Always give thanks to God the Father for everything in the Name of our Lord Jesus Christ. (Eph.5:19-20/NIV)	"I will sing with my spirit, and I will also sing with my understanding." - Apostle Paul (1 Cor.14:15/NIV)
Reverence for Christ: 21. Submit to one another out of reverence for Christ. (Eph.5:21/NIV)	Be kindly affectionate to one another with *brotherly love,* in honor giving *preference* to one another. (Rom.12:10)

Sing - Jesus Is Worthy Of Your Worship

All of our worship is due only unto Jesus, for He is the Most Holy God. In Heaven, millions of angels and saints of God, along with 24 elders and 4 living creatures, fall prostrate before our God's throne and worship Him who lives forever and ever. They do not rest day or night, saying, *"Holy, Holy, Holy, Lord God Almighty,* who was and is and is to come!" (Rev.4:4-11; 7:9-11)

God Will Never Share His Glory With Anyone: Satan desired God's throne and the worship that is due only unto Him and therefore, was cast out of Heaven. (Matt.4:9; Is.14:12-17)

3. Jews & Gentiles Both Reconciled To God By The Cross Of Christ

*Gentiles Brought Near To God By The Blood of Christ...*Apostle Paul says, "Remember that formerly you who are Gentiles by birth and called "**uncircumcised**" by those (Jews) who call themselves "the circumcision" which is done in the body by human hands;

Remember that at that time *you, gentiles, were separated from Christ*, excluded from citizenship in Israel and foreigners to the covenants of the promise, without hope and *without God in the world*. (Eph.2:11-13/NIV)

*Mystery of Christ revealed...*Now the mystery of Christ has been revealed that the Jews and Gentiles are one in Jesus Christ and the gentiles should be fellow heirs, of the same body, and partakers of God's promise in Christ through the Gospel. (Eph.3:3-6)

COMMANDMENT OF GOD FOR US TO OBEY	REWARDS FOR OBEDIENCE/ SUPPORTING SCRIPTURES
To The Gentile Believers: Do not be strangers and foreigners any longer, but *fellow citizens with the saints* and members of the household of God.—Apostle Paul. (Eph.2:19)	*As Gentile Believers, in Christ Jesus,* 1. You are no longer strangers from the *covenants of promise*. (Eph. 2:12) 2. You are now *with hope* and *with God* in the world. (Eph. 2:12) 3. You, who once were far off, *are brought near by the blood of Christ*. (Eph. 2:13) 4. For *Christ Himself is our peace*, who has made both (Jews and Gentiles) one and has *broken down the middle wall of separation*. (Eph.2:14)

COMMANDMENT OF GOD FOR US TO OBEY	REWARDS FOR OBEDIENCE/ SUPPORTING SCRIPTURES
To The Gentile Believers: Do not be strangers and foreigners any longer, but *fellow citizens with the saints* and members of the household of God.—Apostle Paul. (Eph.2:19)	5. For Christ has *abolished in His flesh the enmity*, so as to create in Himself **one new man** *from the two* (Jews and Gentiles), *thus making peace.* (Eph.2:15) 6. For Christ has *reconciled them both to God* in one body through the cross, thereby putting to death the enmity. (Eph.2:16) 7. For through Christ, we *both (Jews & Gentiles) have access by one Spirit to the Father.* (Eph.2:18) 8. Now you, gentiles, are being *built on the foundation of the apostles and prophets*, Jesus Christ Himself being the chief cornerstone. (Eph.2:20) 9. For in Christ, the chief cornerstone, the whole building, being fitted together, grows into a holy temple in the Lord, in whom you, (gentiles) also are being built together for *a dwelling place of God in the Spirit.*—Apostle Paul. (Eph.2:21-22) 10. *The mystery of Christ* is that the *gentiles* should be *fellow heirs* of the same body and *partakers of God's promise* in Christ through the gospel. (Eph.3:4-6)

Every believer in Christ, other than the Jews, is called a gentile believer.

3.1. Preach The Unsearchable Riches Of Christ

Christ ascended far above all the heavens, that *He might fill all things*. And in Christ, *we live and move and have our being*. (Eph.4:10; Acts 17:28)

COMMANDMENTS OF GOD FOR US TO OBEY	REWARDS FOR OBEDIENCE/ SUPPORTING SCRIPTURES
1. Preach the *unsearchable riches of Christ.* (Eph.3:8)	i. For God *created all things through Jesus Christ.* (Eph.3:9)
2. Make all see the *fellowship of the mystery of Christ,* as Apostle Paul did. (Eph.3:9)	ii. God's intent is that now the *manifold wisdom of God* might be *made known by the church* to the principalities and *powers in the heavenly places*; according to the *eternal purpose* which God accomplished in Christ Jesus our Lord. (Eph.3:10-11)
	iii. For we have *boldness and access to God with confidence* through faith in Christ.—Apostle Paul. (Eph.3:12)

The mystery of Christ is that God purposed in His heart to bring all people, both Jews and Gentiles into salvation through faith in Jesus Christ. (Eph.3:6)

3.2. Eternal Purpose of God Through Christ Revealed To The Heavenly Hosts By The Church

*The principalities and powers in heavenly places...*This may refer to good angels or demonic spirits.

The angels in heaven now understand that God's eternal purpose in sending His only begotten Son, Jesus Christ to earth was *to redeem all of mankind (Jews & Gentiles) through His sacrifice on the cross.* All of heaven marvels at this manifold wisdom of God as He demonstrates that wisdom through the church. (Eph.2:15-22; 3:4-12; Col.1:16)

The principalities and powers in heavenly places may also refer to the ruling powers of darkness in the spiritual realm to whom God's eternal purpose is being made known that God has accomplished the *redemption plan through the cross of Christ* to save all of mankind, *as the churches proclaim this salvation message of Jesus Christ* all over the world. (Eph.6:12-18; 2 Cor.10:4-5)

Apostle Paul, A Great Prayer Warrior –
In Prison For Christ

Rembrandt pinx.   A.Böttger sculps.

4. Pray As Apostle Paul Prayed

The prayer of Apostle Paul indicates *God's highest desire* for every believer in Christ.

Paul did not pray for the personal needs of believers; rather he prayed that they should walk in the fullness of the Spirit. From his prayers, we learn that we also should *pray more for the things of the above* than for the earthly things, like house, car, career, etc.

Apostle Paul says...

"Join together in following my example, brothers and sisters, and just as you have *us as a model,* keep your eyes on those who live as we do." (Phil.3:17)

"Be ye followers of me, even as I also am of Christ." (1 Cor.11:1/KJV)

"Put it into practice - whatever you have *learned, or received or heard* from me, or *seen in me."* (Phil 4:9/NIV)

Therefore let us follow Apostle Paul's example and pray as he prayed.

4.1. Pray For The Spirit Of Wisdom & Revelation In the Knowledge of God

COMMANDMENTS OF GOD FOR US TO OBEY	REWARD FOR OBEDIENCE
Pray that the God of our Lord Jesus Christ, the Father of glory, may give to you— i. the Spirit of wisdom and ii. Revelation in the knowledge of Him, as apostle Paul prayed. (Eph.1:16-17)	So that you may **know Him better.** (Eph.1:17/NIV)

Fools Despise The Wisdom of God

- *Fear of God, Beginning of Knowledge:* The fear of God is the beginning of knowledge, but fools despise wisdom and instruction. (Prov.2:7)

- *Fear of God, Beginning of Wisdom:* The fear of God is the beginning of wisdom; a good *understanding* have all those who *do His commandments.* (Ps.111:10)

- *Wisdom of this world is foolishness with God:* Pray for the spirit of *"Reverential Fear of God"* to come upon you and your children. All the degrees you obtain academically in the world are absolutely nothing in the eyes of God; for the wisdom of this world is *foolishness with God.* It is written, "He catches the wise in their own craftiness" and again, "The Lord knows the thoughts of the wise, that they are *futile."* (1 Cor.3:19-20; Is.11:2)

- *Treasure 'My Commands' to Receive Wisdom:* "My son, treasure My commands within you so that you incline your ear to wisdom, and apply your heart to understanding." (Prov.2:1-2)

- *To find the Knowledge of God:*

    i.   Cry out for discernment.
    ii. Lift up your voice for understanding.
    iii. Seek wisdom as silver and
    iv. Search for wisdom as for hidden treasures.

    Then you will *understand the fear of the Lord*, and find the knowledge of God. (Prov.2:3-5)

- *Ask God Persistently for Wisdom:* If any of you lacks wisdom, let him ask of God, who gives to all liberally and without reproach, and it will be given to him. (Jas.1:5)

- *Wisdom only for the Upright:* The Lord stores up sound wisdom for the upright; He is a shield to those who walk uprightly. (Prov.2:7)

- ***When wisdom enters your heart & Knowledge is pleasant to your soul:***

    i. Discretion will **preserve you**;

    ii. Understanding will keep you to **deliver you** from the way of evil -

    - from the man who speaks *perverse* things,
    - from those who leave the paths of uprightness to walk in the ways of *darkness*;
    - from those who rejoice in doing evil,
    - from those who delight in the **perversity of the wicked**;
    - from those whose ways are *crooked*,
    - from those who are *devious* in their paths.

    iii. ***To deliver you from the immoral woman -***

    - from the seductress who flatters with her words,
    - who forsakes the companion of her youth (husband), and
    - who forgets the marriage covenant of her God.

For *her house leads down to death*, and her paths to the dead; none who go to her return, nor do they regain the paths of life. (Prov.2:10-19)

- **Blessings through Wisdom:** When wisdom delivers you from evil men and adulterous women -

  i. You will walk in the way of *goodness.*

  ii. Keep to the paths of *righteousness.*

  iii. For the upright will *dwell in the land.*

  iv. And the blameless will *remain in the land.* (Prov.2:20-21)

- **Consequences for Despising God's Wisdom:**

  i. The wicked, who walk in their own wisdom, will be *cut off from the earth.*

  ii. And the unfaithful to God will be *uprooted from the earth.* (Prov.2:22)

- **Wisdom is a defense, as money is a defense**, but the excellence of knowledge is that wisdom gives *abundant life* on earth and *eternal life* in Heaven, to those who have it. (Ecc.7:12)

4.2. Pray That Your Spiritual Eyes Be Opened

"Blessed are your eyes for they see," said the Lord Jesus to His disciples. (Matt.13:16)

COMMANDMENT OF GOD FOR US TO OBEY	REWARDS FOR OBEDIENCE
Pray that the eyes of your heart be enlightened, as apostle Paul prayed. (Eph.1:18/NIV)	In order that you may know... i. what is the *hope of His calling,* ii. what are the *riches of His glorious inheritance* in the saints and iii. what is the *exceeding greatness of His power toward us* who believe. (Eph.1:18-19)

Points to Ponder:

• The Lord says, "Call to Me, and I will answer you, and *show you great and mighty things,* which you do not know." (Jer.33:3)

• The Sovereign Lord has promised,

   i. "I will pour out *My Spirit on all flesh;*

   ii. Your sons and your daughters shall prophesy,

   iii. Your old men shall dream dreams,

   iv. Your *young men shall see visions.*

   v. And also on My menservants and on My maidservants, I will pour out My Spirit in those days (last days)." (Joel 2:28-29)

Claim these promises of the Lord.

4.3. Pray To Be Strengthened By The Holy Spirit

COMMANDMENT OF GOD FOR US TO OBEY	REWARDS FOR OBEDIENCE
Pray that out of His glorious riches, God may **strengthen you with power through His Spirit in your inner being,** as apostle Paul prayed. (Eph.3:16/NIV)	So that **Christ may dwell in your hearts** through faith.—Apostle Paul. (Eph.3:17/NIV)

Points to Ponder:

- *Spirit Without Measure...*Our Lord has promised, "In the last days *I will pour out My Spirit upon all flesh.*" God is willing to anoint us with His precious Holy Spirit, not only up to our ankles or knees or waist but to the overflowing of our hearts.

  All we need to do is to desperately cry out for the power of the Holy Spirit to be an overcomer. (Ezek.47:1-12; Joel 2:28)

- *Power to Overcome Sin Offered only by Jesus:* All religions teach good morals; for example, walk in love, forgive one another, do not steal, etc. but only our Lord Jesus offers us the power and the presence of the Holy Spirit, to overcome sin, Satan and the world. Make use of the power of the Holy Spirit that is available to you to have a victorious life.

❖ If you have **never fallen into the sin of addiction**, such as, alcoholism, smoking, drug use, sexual immorality, etc. and have overcome sin by the power of the Holy Spirit, like Jesus - **this victorious life is more of a testimony** of the saving grace of Jesus, *than Jesus saving you from your wretched, sinful lifestyle*, in His grace. Hence, strive to be an overcomer at any cost.

4.4. Pray To Comprehend Christ's Love For You

COMMANDMENTS OF GOD FOR US TO OBEY	REWARDS FOR OBEDIENCE/ SUPPORTING SCRIPTURES
1. *Pray that, being rooted and established in love...* i. you may have **power,** together with all the saints, *to grasp how wide and long and high and deep is the love of Christ,* and ii. you may *know* this love that surpasses knowledge, as apostle Paul prayed. (Eph.3:17-19/NIV)	i. So that you may be *filled with all the fullness of God.* (Eph.3:19) ii. For God is *able to do exceedingly abundantly above all* that we *ask or think,* according to the *power* that works in us. (Eph.3:20) iii. Now *to God be glory in the church* and in Christ Jesus to all generations *forever and ever.* (Eph.3:21)
Let your love abound more and more... 2. Pray that your love may abound more and more in knowledge and *depth of insight,* as Apostle Paul prayed. (Phil. 1:9/NIV)	*So that...* i. you may be able to *discern what is best;* ii. you may be *pure and blameless* until the day of Christ; and iii. you may be filled with the *fruit of righteousness* that comes through Jesus Christ—to the glory and praise of God. (Phil. 1:10-11/NIV)

"Love One Another As I Have Loved You"

Jesus says, "A new commandment I give unto you, that you love one another as I have loved you." (Jn.13:34)

The characteristics of true love -

1. Love is **patient.**
2. Love is **kind.**
3. Love does **not envy.**
4. Love is **not proud**.
5. Love is **not rude**.
6. Love is **not self-seeking**.
7. Love is **not easily angered**.

8. Love **keeps no record of wrongs**.
9. Love **thinks no evil**.
10. Love **bears all things**.
11. Love believes all things.
12. Love **endures all** things
13. Love **never fails**.
14. Though we **give all** we possess to the poor but **have not love**, we gain **nothing in Heaven**.
15. God values genuine love greater than ministry, faith or spiritual gifts. Love is the greatest of faith, hope and love. (1 Cor.13:3-8,13)
16. **Love covers all sins.** (Prov.10:12)

How do we receive this "Christ-like love"?

It is poured out into our hearts **by the Holy Spirit**, as we wait on Him. (Rom.5:5)

4.5. Grace To All Who Love Our Lord Jesus Christ With An Undying Love!

• *Everlasting Love of God…* The Lord says, "I have loved you with an everlasting love; therefore **with loving kindness I have drawn you**." (Jer.31:3)
• *The unconditional love of Jesus…Jesus loves you so much* that He died in your place and took the penalty of your sins upon Himself. He loves you just as you are.
• *"Remain in My Love"*…Jesus says, "*As the Father has loved Me*, so have *I loved you*. Now remain in My love." (Jn.15:9/NIV)
• *Your deep love for Christ…*First you should comprehend how wide and long and high and deep is Christ's love for you, then you must pray that your love for Christ may abound more and more.
• *Your passion for Christ will make you live a holy life….*When you have an undying love for your Bridegroom, Jesus Christ, then you will desire to live a righteous, pure and blameless life until you meet Him face to face; for you will never want to grieve His loving heart.

• *"If you love Me, keep My Commandments,"* says Jesus. If you truly love the Lord Jesus, then it will be easy for you to obey His Commandments. (Jn.14:15)

4.6. Pray To Be Filled With The Knowledge Of God's Will

Jesus warns: "Not everyone who says to Me, 'Lord, Lord,' shall **enter the Kingdom of Heaven,** but **he who does the will of My Father** in heaven. Many will say to Me in that day, 'Lord, Lord, have we not prophesied in Your name, cast out demons in Your name, and done many wonders in Your name?' And then I will declare to them, **'I never knew you; depart from Me, you who practice lawlessness!'** (Matt.7:21-23)

COMMANDMENTS OF GOD FOR US TO OBEY	REWARDS FOR OBEDIENCE/ SUPPORTING SCRIPTURES
1. Pray that you may be filled with the knowledge of God's will in all wisdom and spiritual understanding, as Apostle Paul prayed. (Col.1:9)	So that... i. You may live a **life worthy of the Lord,** (Col. 1:10/NIV) ii. You may **please Him in every way.** (Col. 1:10/NIV) iii. You may **bear fruit** in every good work. (Col. 1:10/NIV) iv. You may **grow in the knowledge of God.** (Col. 1:10/NIV) v. You may **be strengthened with all power** according to His glorious might, so that you may **have great endurance and patience.**—Apostle Paul (Col. 1:11/NIV)
2. You, **joyfully give thanks** to the Father, as Apostle Paul did. (Col. 1:12/NIV)	i. For God has qualified you to share in the **inheritance of the saints** in the Kingdom of light. (Col. 1:12/NIV) ii. For God has **rescued you from the dominion of darkness** and brought you into the Kingdom of the Son He loves.—Apostle Paul. (Col. 1:13/NIV) iii. In Christ, you have **redemption,** the forgiveness of sins. (Col. 1:14/NIV)

4.7. Pray That You May Be Encouraged In Heart

COMMANDMENT OF GOD FOR US TO OBEY	REWARDS FOR OBEDIENCE/
Pray that you may be encouraged in heart and united in love. - Apostle Paul (Col.2:2/NIV)	1. So that you may have the *full riches* of *complete understanding.* (Col.2:2/NIV)
	2. In order that you may *know the mystery of God, namely, Christ,* in whom are *hidden all the treasures* of wisdom and knowledge. (Col.2:2-3/NIV)
	3. So that *no one may deceive you* by fine-sounding arguments.— Apostle Paul (Col.2:4/NIV)

Points to Ponder...

* *Be Encouraged in Heart:* Strengthen your inner man...

  i. by having *intimate relationship with Christ* through prayer

  ii. by meditating on the *Word of God*

  iii. by *obeying the Commandments of God* and

  iv. by the *infilling of the Holy Spirit*

  v. so that you will *understand the fullness of Jesus Christ,* the mystery of God, in whom all the treasures of wisdom and knowledge are hidden.

* *Be united in love...*Apostle Paul is exhorting the believers to be united in love and to edify one another in faith so that we can grow together in the complete understanding of who Christ is and how good and loving God is.

* Then you will not be deceived by the enticing words of men. (Col.2:1-7)

5. Submit To One Another In The Fear Of God

Commandments regarding the following topics will enable you to have a Godly, healthy family unit:

- Children, Honor Your Father & Mother To Enjoy Long Life
- Husband & Wife - One Flesh, A Profound Mystery
- God Instituted Marriage Between A Man & A Woman
- Servants & Masters - Remember, Your Master is in Heaven!

*Godly family...*God has established the family as the basic unit in society. Mutual submission in Christ is an important spiritual principle that every Christian family should follow.

In order to live the abundant life intended by the Lord God Almighty, each member of the family must exhibit the characteristics of *submission, humility, gentleness, patience and respect for each other.*

5.1. Children, Honor Your Father & Mother To Enjoy Long Life

COMMANDMENTS OF GOD FOR US TO OBEY	REWARDS FOR OBEDIENCE/ SUPPORTING SCRIPTURES
1. Children, *Obey* your parents in the Lord. (Eph.6:1/NIV)	For this is right. (Eph.6:1)
2. *Honor* your father and mother. (Eph.6:2/NIV)	For this is the first commandment with the promise that - i. it may *go well with you* and ii. you may *enjoy long life* on the earth. (Eph.6:2-3/NIV)
To The Fathers... 3. *Fathers,* do not provoke your children to wrath.(Eph.6:4)	Instead, bring them up in the training and instruction of the Lord. (Eph.6:4/NIV)

• Children should honor and obey their father and mother since *parents are the pride of children.* (Prov.17:6)

❖ **Parents, Pray fervently over your sons & daughters, for them to receive...**

i. Spirit of Conviction & Repentance of sin. (Jn.14:15-17; Is.59:1-2; Lk.13:1-5)

ii. Spirit of Reverential Fear of God. (Is.11:2)

iii. Spirit of Obedience to God's commandments. (Matt.5:19; Matt.28:20)

iv. Spirit of Humility. (Matt.5:5; Lk.18:14)

v. Fire of the Holy Spirit (Jn.3:13-18)

vi. Spirit of Wisdom & Understanding. (Is.11:1-2)

vii. Spirit of Counsel & Might. (Is.11:1-2)

viii. Spirit of Knowledge & Revelation. (Is.11:1-2; Eph.1:16-17; Jer.33:3)

ix. Visions & Dreams (Joel 2:28; Jer.33:3)

x. 9 Fruits & 9 Gifts of the Holy Spirit (Gal.5:22-23; 1 Cor.12:4-11)

5.2. Husband & Wife–One Flesh, A Profound Mystery

COMMANDMENTS OF GOD FOR US TO OBEY	REWARDS FOR OBEDIENCE/ SUPPORTING SCRIPTURES
Wives... 1. Wives, submit to your own husbands, as to the Lord. (Eph.5:22) 2. Wives, respect your husbands. (Eph.5:33/NIV)	i. For the husband is the head of the wife, *as Christ is the head of the church,* His body, of which He is the Savior. (Eph.5:23/NIV) ii. Now *as the church submits to Christ,* so also wives should submit to their husbands in everything. (Eph.5:24/NIV)

- A man will leave his father and mother and be united to his wife. And the *two will become one flesh.* This is a *profound mystery* about *Christ and the church.* (Eph.5:31-32/NIV)

- *Wife's Commitment In Marriage:*

  1. *Be a Helper...*The wife should be a help-mate to her husband. (Gen.2:18)

  2. *Submit in Love...*The wife should love her husband and submit to him in everything, as unto the Lord; as the church submits to Christ. (Eph.5:22-24)

  3. *Good attitude...*The wife can win her unsaved husband for the Lord, by her good behavior without any talk. (1 Pet.3:1)

  4. *Be gracious...*Who can find a wife of **noble character**? She is **worth far more than Rubies**. A wife should be a woman of noble character.

  5. *Be God-Fearing...*A wife must have the fear of God to be worthy of her husband's praise. (Prov.31:10-31)

COMMANDMENTS OF GOD FOR US TO OBEY	REWARDS FOR OBEDIENCE/ SUPPORTING SCRIPTURES
Husbands...	*How to love your wife?*
1. Husbands, love your wives, just as Christ loved the church. (Eph.5:25/NIV)	*1. As Christ loved the Church...* i. For *Christ gave Himself up for the church* to make her holy, ii. cleansing the church by the washing with water through the Word, iii. and *to present her to Himself* as a radiant church, without stain or wrinkle or any other blemish, but *holy and blameless.* (Eph.5:25-27/NIV) 2. In this same way, husbands ought to love their wives *as their own bodies.* (Eph.5:28/NIV) 3. Each one of you must love his wife *as he loves himself.* (Eph.5:33/NIV)
2. Husbands, love your wives as your own bodies. (Eph.5:28/NIV) 3. Each one of you *must love* his wife as he loves himself. (Eph.5:33/NIV)	i. For *He who loves his wife loves himself.* (Eph.5:28/NIV) ii. After all, *no one ever hated his own body*, but he feeds and cares for it; iii. just *as Christ does the church—* for we are members of His body. (Eph.5:29-30/NIV)
4. Leave your father and mother and be united to your wife. (Eph.5:31/NIV)	And the two of *you will become one flesh.* (Eph.5:31/NIV) This is a *profound mystery* about Christ and the church. (Eph.5:31-32/NIV)

- *Husband's Commitment In Marriage:*

1. **Treat Your Wife with Respect & Honor**...Husbands ought to treat their wives with respect and honor and as equal heirs of God's gracious gift of life, so that their prayers may not be hindered. (1 Pet.3:7)

2. **Treat Your Wife as Equal**...Since Eve was taken from the rib of Adam, from his side and not from his head or his feet, the wife should be treated as equal with her husband and not above him or under his feet. (Gen.2:22)

3. **Appreciate** the noble character and the goodness of your wife. (Prov.31:10-31)

4. **Praise the woman who Fears the Lord;** for charm is deceptive and beauty is vain. (Prov.31:30)

5.3. God Ordained Marriage

I. *God's way:*

God instituted the traditional marriage, which is a *covenant between a man and a woman, with God as witness*. (Mal.2:12-15)

Examples of Traditional Marriages in the Bible...

1. God created the first man, *Adam,* in His own image and gave him a *wife named Eve*. (Gen.1:26-27; 2:22-24; 3:20)

2. God called *Abraham, the father of faith,* out of idolatry, along with his *wife, Sarah*. (Gen.12:5)

3. God chose a beautiful *wife named Rebecca for Isaac*. (Gen.24:67)

4. God called *Mary and her husband, Joseph,* to fulfill His will of being Jesus' parents. (Matt.1:18-19)

5. *Zecharias and his wife, Elizabeth,* were parents to John, the Baptist, the forerunner of Jesus Christ. (Lk.1:5; 57-60)

II. *Our Way Based on God's Way:*

As believers in Christ, we should follow God's way and marry only another believer in Christ, build a family unit and raise up godly children.

5.4. God Intends Your Life Partner To Be Your Helper

Lessons from the "First Marriage" ordained by God...

I. God's Way:

- *Adam was all alone and did not find a suitable companion...* When God created Adam, he was all alone in the Garden of Eden since he did not find a helper comparable to him *from amongst all of God's creation.* (Gen.2:18-20)

- *God chose a female companion for Adam...*God said, "It is not good that man should be alone." So God decided to give Adam a suitable *female helper for companionship and intimacy, to have godly offspring.* (Gen.2:18; Mal.2:12-15)

- *God made Eve from Adam...*When God made Eve from out of Adam and brought her to him, Adam said: "This is now *bone of my bones and flesh of my flesh;* she shall be called Woman because she was taken out of Man." *God saw them as one flesh.* (Gen.2:21-24)

II. Our Way Based on God's Way:

- *Thank God, You Have a Life Partner...* Think of the times when you were lonely in your life like Adam was, and now if God has blessed you with a partner, be thankful to God. If not, pray to God for a suitable partner.

- *Husband and Wife, One Flesh...*In a marital relationship, husband and wife should join together and become one flesh and love and care for each other. (Gen.2:24)

- *Pride is the Cause for Strife...* Be faithful to your partner and enjoy your life together by treating each other well; for *only by pride comes contention.* (Prov.13:10)

- *Mend Your Troubled Marriage...* If your marriage is in trouble because of attitude problems, you should work it out amicably with God's help. Divorce is not an option; for *God hates divorce.* (Mal.2:16)

5.5. Simple Wedding Is God's Choice

I. *God's Way:*

- Scripture says that after making **the woman, God brought her to Adam** and gave her to be his wife. (Gen.2:21-24)

- If God had desired to celebrate Adam and Eve's wedding with grandeur, He could have invited all of His heavenly hosts, the angels, and He could have decorated the Garden of Eden and had an elaborate celebration.

- There was a reason for God to celebrate since it was the first wedding on earth, yet He chose to have a simple wedding for the first couple on earth.

II. *Our Way Based On God's Way:*

- You need not follow the ways of the world and imitate what people around you do.

- Don't be sad if you cannot have a grand wedding, as long as God is in it.

Pray & Find Your Soul Mate

5.6. Godly Counsel To The Unmarried

Finding Your Soul Mate

Partner of God's Choice: It is better to pray and find a life partner of God's choice, for marriage is a turning point in your life. But you must be willing to accept whoever God chooses for you, regardless of his/her financial status, qualification, family background, etc.

God will Reveal Your Soul-mate to you: When you sincerely pray to God to find your soul-mate, God may speak to you audibly, through His Word, through visions and dreams, through the Servants of God, etc., and show you whom He has specifically chosen for you.

Believe that God will only give you what is best for you: When you accept God's choice joyfully, then He will bring the best out of your life; for God knows the end from the beginning. For example, Abraham's servant prayed to find a suitable bride for his master's son, Isaac, and God answered his prayer favorably. Isaac cheerfully accepted God's choice, Rebecca, as his bride and fulfilled God's will, in bringing the nation of *Israel into existence,* through his generation. *Jesus, our Savior, was born in his lineage.* Isaac was **blessed beyond measure** for his obedience. (Gen.24:12-14)

★ *At the age of 26, I fervently prayed for 6 months to find a life partner. God showed me 100%, through His Word, whom I should marry. I got married to the man of God's choice, under whom God prepared me for my calling.*

When we cheerfully accept God's choice, God can mold us to fulfill His purpose for our lives. – Author

• *"Living Together"* outside of marriage is not Biblical and it is adultery in the eyes of God. Sexual relationships before marriage are also forbidden by God. (Matt.5:28-30; Gen.29:15-28)

• A Christian should marry only another believer in Christ and never a heathen. Do not get into a relationship because of infatuation. It will divert you from fulfilling God's Will for your life. (2 Cor.6:14-16; Eph.1:3-12)

• Perversion and same sex marriage are an abomination before God. (1 Cor.6:9-10)

• Hebrews 13:4 says, "Marriage should be **honored** by all, and marriage **bed kept pure.**" So guard your *virginity* at any cost till you are married.

5.7. Servants & Masters–Remember, Your Master is in Heaven

COMMANDMENTS OF GOD FOR US TO OBEY	REWARDS FOR OBEDIENCE/ SUPPORTING SCRIPTURES
Servants... 1. **Be obedient** to those who are your masters according to the flesh, i. with fear and trembling, ii. in sincerity of heart, iii. **as to Christ;** iv. not with eye service, as men pleasers. (Eph.6:5-6)	*Be obedient as servants of Christ...* i. **doing the will of God** from the heart, ii. **with goodwill** doing service, iii. **as to the Lord,** iv. *and* **not to men.** (Eph.6:6-7)
2. **Serve wholeheartedly,** as if you were serving the Lord, not men. (Eph.6:7/NIV)	Because you know that the **Lord will reward everyone for whatever good they do,** whether they are slave or free. (Eph.6:8/NIV)
Masters... 3. Treat your slaves as if you were serving the Lord, not men. 4. Do not threaten them. (Eph.6:9/NIV)	i. Since you know that God who is both **their master and yours is in Heaven**. ii. There is **no favoritism with Him**. (Eph.6:9/NIV)

6. Salvation, The Gift Of God & Not Of Your Works

COMMANDMENT OF GOD FOR US TO OBEY	REWARDS FOR OBEDIENCE/ SUPPORTING SCRIPTURES
For the gentiles:	1. For *it is the gift of God.* (Eph. 2:8)
By grace, you *be saved through faith in Christ,* and not of yourselves and not of works, lest you should boast. - Apostle Paul (Eph.2:7-9)	2. For God, who is *rich in mercy,* because of *His great love* with which He loved us, even when you *are dead in trespasses...*
	i. *He makes you alive together with Christ.* (Eph.2:4-5)
	ii. He *raises you* up. (Eph.2:6)
	iii. He makes you *sit together in the heavenly places* in Christ Jesus. (Eph.2:6)
	3. So that in the ages to come God might *show the exceeding riches of His grace* in *His* kindness toward us (believers) in Christ Jesus.— Apostle Paul (Eph. 2:7)

- Scripture says, "All have sinned and fall short of the glory of God; the *wages of sin is death,* but the gift of God is eternal life in Christ our Lord." (Rom.3:23; 6:23)

- *Sin cannot be nullified,* once committed. Your Salvation cannot be bought with money, even with billions of dollars, nor by doing good works but only through faith in Christ. It is the *"Gift of God."* (Eph.2:8-9)

- ★ *I stood in the gap for my dad's salvation for 19 years. I just would not let my dad go to hellfire for eternity. Finally, at the age of 79, the day after my dad accepted Jesus as his Savior, the Lord took him home to Heaven. So **do not give up on your unsaved family members** and relatives. No one else on earth can intercede for their salvation as much as you can. (Ezek.22:30) – Author*

Put On the Whole Armor of God

7. Take Your Stand Against The Devil's Schemes

Put On The Whole Armor Of God

COMMANDMENTS OF GOD FOR US TO OBEY	REWARDS FOR OBEDIENCE/ SUPPORTING SCRIPTURES
1. Be strong in the Lord and in His mighty power. (Eph.6:10/NIV) 2. Put on the whole armor of God. (Eph.6:11)	So that you can take your stand against the devil's schemes. (Eph.6:11/NIV)
What Is The Whole Armor Of God? 3. Stand firm ... i. with the **belt of truth** buckled around your waist, ii. with the **breastplate of righteousness** in place, iii. and with your *feet* fitted with the readiness that comes from the *gospel of peace.* iv. Take up the **shield of faith**, with which you can extinguish all the flaming arrows of the evil one. v. Take the **helmet of salvation**. vi. Take the **sword of the Spirit**, which is the Word of God. (Eph.6:14-17/NIV)	*Why Should We Put On The Whole Armor of God?* For our struggle is... i. not against flesh and blood, ii. but against the **rulers**, iii. against the **authorities**, iv. against the **powers of this dark world** v. and against the **spiritual forces of evil** in the heavenly realms. (Eph.6:12/NIV)

COMMANDMENTS OF GOD FOR US TO OBEY	REWARDS FOR OBEDIENCE/ SUPPORTING SCRIPTURES
4. Take up the whole armor of God. (Eph.6:13)	So that you may be able *to withstand in the evil day,* and having done all, to stand. (Eph.6:13)
5. *Pray in the Spirit on all occasions* with all kinds of prayers and requests. (Eph.6:18/NIV)	i. You, beloved, *build yourselves up* on your most holy faith, *praying in the Holy Spirit.* (Jude 1:20) ii. For he who speaks in the Spirit, *speaks mysteries with God.* (1 Cor.14:2, 4)
6. Be alert and always *keep on praying* for all the saints. (Eph.6:18/NIV)	For our struggle is not against flesh and blood but against the spiritual forces of evil. (Eph.6:12/NIV)

Our Spiritual Warfare

- Ephesians 6:12 says,

  i. We wrestle not against flesh and blood (human beings),

  ii. but against **principalities**, and

  iii. **powers of darkness,**

  iv. against the **rulers** of the darkness of this world,

  v. against **spiritual wickedness** in high places.

- Jesus declared, "Behold, I give you the **authority** to trample on serpents and scorpions, and over **all the power of the enemy (Satan),** and nothing shall by any means hurt you." (Lk.10:19)

7.1. Jesus Gives You Authority Over Satan

1. **Jesus has all authority...**Jesus proclaimed, "All authority has been given to Me in heaven and on earth." (Matt.28:18)

2. **Jesus gives us, believers, the authority over Satan...** Jesus declared, 'Behold, I give you the authority over all the power of the enemy.' (Lk.10:19)

3. **How do we use the authority over Satan?**

   • **Bind the strong man, Satan...**Jesus said, First bind the strong man and **then you plunder his house.** (Matt.12:28-29)

   • "Assuredly, I say to you, **whatever you bind on earth will be bound** in heaven." (Matt.18:18)

   • **Resist the devil...**Submit to God. Resist the devil and **he will flee** from you. (Jas. 4:7)

   • **Crush the mountains of Satan...**The Lord says, "Behold, I will make you into a new threshing sledge with sharp teeth; You shall thresh the mountains (of Satan) and beat *them* small, and make the hills like chaff." (Is.41:15)

   • **Greater is He who is in you...**You can join with another believer and bind the devil; for He, the Holy Spirit, who is in you is greater than he, the devil, who is in the world. (1 Jn.4:4; Lk.10:19)

   • **Wait on the Lord** to be empowered by the Holy Spirit. (Ps.27:14; Is.40:31)

4. **What are the ways to overcome Satan?**

   o By the Name of Jesus (Matt.28:18; Phil.2:9; Eph.1:20-23)

   o By the Blood of Jesus (Rev.12:11)

   o By the Word of our Testimony (Rev.12:11)

   o By the Word of God (Matt.4)

   o By the power of the Holy Spirit (Matt.12:28; 1 Cor.6:19)

   o By fasting and fervent prayer (Matt.17:21)

   o By rejoicing and praising God (Josh.6:20)

5. **Why should we bind Satan?**

- Remember, Satan comes to steal, to kill and to destroy; for he is the enemy of our souls. (Jn.10:10)

- Satan is a deceiver, who snares you into sin. Satan's latest strategy is to do *"Psycho War,"* instilling filthy and lustful or murderous and destructive thoughts in our minds. Be watchful!

6. **Which evil spirits should we bind?**

Jesus said to those who believe in Him –"In My Name, you shall cast out devils." (Mk.16:17)

Following are some of the evil spirits which you should bind and cast out:

Spirit of Lust & Perversion	*Spirit of Depression*
Spirit of Pornography	Spirit of Heaviness
Spirit of Adultery	Spirit of Despair
Spirit of Fornication	Spirit of Emptiness
Spirit of Prostitution	Spirit of Self-pity
Spirit of Theft	Negative Spirit
Spirit of Anger	*Spirit of Suicide*
Spirit of Violence	*Mind-blinding Spirit*
Spirit of Murder	Spirit of Confusion
Spirit of Hatred	*Spirit of Pride*
Spirit of Vengeance	Spirit of Greed
Spirit of Envy	Spirit of Selfishness
Spirit of Destruction	*Judgmental Spirit*
Spirit of Death	
Spirit of Unforgiveness	Spirit of Contempt
Spirit of Bitterness	*Spirit of Strife*
	Spirit of Discontent
Spirit of Fear	*Spirit of Murmur*
Spirit of Unbelief	

Spirit of Timidity	*Spirit of Antichrist*
Spirit of Anxiety	Spirit of Blasphemy
Spirit of Idolatry	*Jezebel Spirit*
Spirit of Deception	Spirit of Hypocrisy
Spirit of Lies	*Spirit of Vanity*
Spirit of Persecution	*Spirit of Worldliness*
Spirit of Opposition	Spirit of Self-righteousness
Dominating Spirit	*Spirit of Infirmity*
Spirit of Rebellion	Deaf and Dumb Spirit
Tormenting Spirit	*Religious Spirit*
Devouring Spirit	Legalistic Spirit
Accusing Spirit	Familiar Spirit
Spirit of Resistance	Spirit of Divination
Spirit of Disobedience	Spirit of Sorcery
Spirit of Guilt	*Spirit of Witchcraft*
Spirit of Condemnation	Spirit of Addiction
Spirit of Slothfulness	*Spirit of Blindness*
Spirit of Stinginess	*Spirit of Division*
Spirit of Poverty	*Spirit of Racism*

Ref. Verses: Gal.5:19-21; Is.19:14; Prov.17:20; Matt.5:28; 1 Cor.6:9-10; Rom.1:26-28; 1 Jn.3:15; 1 Tim.6:9; Is.59:7; Ex.12:29; 2 Kings 19:35; 1 Jn.3:8; Matt.5:22; Ps.37:8-9; Matt.6:15; Heb.12:15; Rom.12:19; 1 Pet.2:1; Rev.2:20;

1 Kings 21:25; Prov.16:18-19; Prov.15:27; 1 Tim.6:10; Matt.7:1-2; Phil.2:3; 1 Tim.6:5-10; 2 Tim.1:7; Jn.3:18-19; Heb.3:16-19; Matt.6:34; Phil.4:6-7; Is.61:3; 2 Cor.4:4; 1 Cor.14:33; Ps.42:5; Ps.51:12; Ecc.7:17; Phil.2:14; Num.14:2;

Rom.8:1; Prov.19:15; Prov.28:22; 1 Kings 22:22; Ps.40:17; Jn.10:10; Matt.23:23; Ecc.1:14; Is.64:6; James 4:4; 1 Jn.2:15; Lk.13:11; Mk.9:25; 1 Jn. 4:1-3; Matt.12:31-32; 1 Sam.15:23; 1 Tim.4:1; Rev.2:10; 1 Sam.16:14; 1 Pet.5:8; Rev.12:10; Rom.13:1-2; Eph.2:1-2; 2 Tim.3:5; Col.2:8; Lev.20:27; Acts 16:16; 2 Kings 21:6; 2 Chr.33:6; 2 Cor.4:4; Prov.20:1; Matt.16:6; 1 Cor.1:10; Prov.24:23

7.2. Ways To Wrestle Against Satan & His Hosts

Submit yourselves first to God; then resist the devil and he will flee from you. (Jas.4:7)

1. **Through the Word of God**: You can resist the devil by quoting Scriptures relevant to the situation. When you meditate on the Word of God daily, you will always be prepared for the spiritual warfare. The "Word" is your weapon. To wrestle against Satan and his hosts, you need to *sharpen your sword* by constantly devouring the Word of God. (Matt.4:4, 6-7; Eph.6:12-17)

2. **Through Jesus' Name,** *the Name above every other name:* You can bind the devil in Jesus' Name and cast him out of your life. For all power is given unto Jesus in Heaven and on earth. (Matt.28:18; Phil.2:9; Eph.1:20-23)

3. **Through the Blood of Jesus:** We overcome the enemy, Satan, by the precious blood of the slain Lamb of God, Jesus Christ, and by the words of our testimony. (Rev.12:11)

4. **Through the Power of the Holy Spirit**: Since you are the temple of the Holy Spirit, He who dwells inside of you will empower you, to take authority over the devil. (Acts 1:8; Lk.10:19)

5. **Through Fervent Prayer & Fasting:** Certain kind of demons cannot be cast out except through prayer and fasting. When we pray, especially in the gift of tongues, God will send forth His angels to fight our battles. Praying in the Spirit will paralyze the enemy quickly. (Matt.17:21; Dan.10:12-14)

6. **Through Shouts of Praise & Joy:** When you praise God with a cheerful heart, He will fight your battles; for He is the Lord of Hosts.

   You can give place to the devil and prolong the trial by talking your fears out; for life and death are in the power of your tongue. (Josh.6; Prov.18:21)

7. **By Binding the evil spirits:** Scripture says, *"Greater is He (Jesus) that is in you,* than he (Satan) that is in the world." (1 Jn.4:4)

Therefore, be bold and take authority over Satan. Bind the evil spirits and cast them out in the name of Jesus; for example, the **spirit of lust**, the spirit of fornication, the spirit of bitterness and **unforgiveness**, etc. (Lk.10:19; Matt.12:29)

8. **By Being Righteous & Obedient to God:** As a soldier in the Lord's army, you need to be 100% holy and righteous before God, to wrestle against Satan effectively; so that the **God of Peace** can **crush Satan under your feet quickly.** (Eph.6:12-17; Rom.16:19-20)

9. ***The Lord of Hosts Fights Your Battles:*** Be encouraged! God sends 2 guardian angels to every believer in Christ (e.g., a little Michael and a little Gabriel). If you have a higher calling, then the Lord may send many more powerful angels to protect you and to fight your spiritual battles against Satan. (Ps.91:11-12; Matt.26:53; Dan.10:4-13)

   ＊ By God's grace, the Lord has gifted me to see my guardian angels. For example, while meditating the Scriptures, if I get a revelation from the Word or when I apply God's Word to a specific situation in my life, I often see my angels fluttering all around me, as though confirming to me that 'I got it.'

   Ask the Lord for the privilege of seeing your guardian angels. (Jer.33:3) - Author

8. Walk Worthy Of Your Calling–Be One In Christ

COMMANDMENTS OF GOD FOR US TO OBEY	REWARDS FOR OBEDIENCE/ SUPPORTING SCRIPTURES
Be One in Christ...	*For there is...*
Walk worthy of the calling with which you were called...	*one Body* (Church) and *one Spirit* (Holy Spirit),
i. with all lowliness,	just as you were called in
ii. gentleness,	*one hope of your calling;*
iii. with long suffering,	*one Lord,*
iv. *bearing with one another in love,*	*one faith,*
v. endeavoring to *keep the unity* of the Spirit in the bond of peace. (Eph.4:1-3)	*one baptism;*
	one God and Father of all, who *is* above all, and through all, and in you all. (Eph.4:4-6)

*Walk in unity...*To walk worthy of your calling and to be one in Christ, you should *be filled with the fruit of the Holy Spirit*, i.e., love, lowliness, gentleness, long suffering, etc. If you seek the Lord with genuine hunger, Jesus will baptize you with His Holy Spirit and fire. (Matt.3:11)

❖ To walk worthy of your calling, plead with the Lord to fill you with the following:

- Spirit of *Reverential Fear of God.* (Is.11:2)
- Spirit of Humility. (Is.57:15)
- Spirit of Conviction & Repentance of sins. (Ps.51:17)
- *Spirit of Obedience* to obey God's Commandments. (Matt.5:19; Jn.14:15)
- Spirit of Surrender & Dependence on God. (Gal.2:20; Rom.8:26)
- Spirit of Prayer & Intercession. (2 Chr.7:14; Ezek.22:30)
- Spirit of the Lord - *7 fold Spirit*. (Is.11:2; Matt.3:11)

9. You Are Made Alive In Christ! You, Who Were Dead In Your Sins

COMMANDMENTS OF GOD FOR US TO OBEY	REWARDS FOR OBEDIENCE/ SUPPORTING SCRIPTURES
1. Be made alive by trusting in Christ, you who are dead in your transgressions and sins. (Eph.2:1; 1:12) 2. Do not walk according to the course of this world. (Eph.2:2) 3. Do not walk according to the prince of the power of the air. (Eph.2:2) 4. Do not be *sons of disobedience.* (Eph.2:2) 5. Do not conduct yourselves in the lusts of your flesh. (Eph.2:3) 6. Do not fulfill the *desires of the flesh* and *of the mind.*—Apostle Paul (Eph.2:3)	i. Or else, you will be *children of wrath.* (Eph.2:3) ii. For the *spirit of the prince of the air (Satan) works* in the sons of disobedience.—Apostle Paul (Eph.2:2)

Pause & Think!

- *Jesus Makes You Alive…*When you accept Christ as your Lord and Savior and develop an intimate relationship with Him daily, He keeps you alive in Him. (Jn.10:10; Acts 17:28; Rom.6:11; Eph.2:5)

- *The Word of God Makes You Alive…*When you meditate on God's Word, His Word revives your soul and keeps you alive. (Ps.19:7)

- *Obeying God's Commandments Makes You Alive…*Everyday as you wait on Him, Christ fills you with His Holy Spirit and helps you obey God's commandments to keep you alive. (Matt.4:4)

- *The Holy Spirit Makes You Alive…*Know the power of the resurrection of Christ which can make alive every dead situation in your life, including your marriage, your family and your sick body. (Rom.8:11)

9.1. Jesus Accepts You Just As You Are

Know Who You Are In Christ & Declare It...

- You are **blessed** with **every spiritual blessing** in Christ. (Eph.1:3)
- You have **citizenship in heaven**. (Phil.3:20)
- You are **seated with Christ** in the heavenly realm. (Eph.2:6)
- You are an **heir of God and joint heir with Christ**. (Rom.8:17)
- You have an **inheritance** in heaven. (Eph.1:11)
- You are **chosen** before the creation of the world **to be holy** and blameless in God's sight. (Eph.1:4)
- You are **predestined** to be adopted as **children of God**. (Eph.1:5)
- You are **adopted** as God's children **to live to His praise**. (Eph.1:6)
- You are freely given God's **glorious grace** in Christ. (Eph.1:6)
- You are **redeemed** through the precious blood of Christ. (Eph.1:7)
- You are **forgiven** in Christ. (Eph.1:7; Col.1:13-14)
- You are **justified** by faith in Christ. (Rom.5:1)
- You are a **new creation** in Christ. (2 Cor.5:17)
- You are the **righteousness of God** in Christ. (2 Cor.5:21)
- You are **free from condemnation** in Christ Jesus, **when you walk according to the Spirit**. (Rom.8:1-2; Gal.5:16)
- You are **made alive** in the Spirit. (1 Pet.3:18)
- You are **complete in Christ**. (Col.2:10)
- You are the **temple of God**. (1 Cor.3:16)
- You have **direct access to the throne of grace**. (Heb.4:14-16)
- You are not given the spirit of fear, but the **Spirit of power and love and a sound mind**. (2 Tim.1:17)
- You are **God's workmanship** created **for good works**. (Eph.2:10)
- You **can do all things through Christ** who strengthens you. (Phil.4:13)
- You are **delivered from the kingdom of darkness** and transferred into the Kingdom of God. (Col.1:13)
- You are **rescued from the coming wrath of God**. (1 Thes.1:10)

Arise & Shine! You Are Precious In God's Eyes

10. You Are Equipped To Be Perfect In Christ

Jesus commands, *"Be perfect as your heavenly Father is perfect."* (Matt.5:48/NIV)

COMMANDMENTS OF GOD FOR US TO OBEY	REWARDS FOR OBEDIENCE/ SUPPORTING SCRIPTURES
1. You should…	*Spiritual Gifts…*
i. *no longer be children,*	1. To each one of us **grace is given** according to the measure of Christ's gift. (Eph.4:7)
ii. tossed to and fro	
iii. and *carried about with every wind of doctrine,*	2. For Christ Himself gave some *to be* **apostles,** some **prophets,** some **evangelists,** and some **pastors** and **teachers…**
iv. by the *trickery of men,*	
v. in the *cunning craftiness* of *deceitful plotting.* (Eph.4:14)	i. for the *equipping* of the saints
	ii. for the **work of ministry,**
2. No longer be a child but be a perfect man. (Eph.4:13-14)	iii. for the *edifying* of the body of Christ,
	iv. till we all come to the **unity of the faith,**
3. Speak the truth in love. (Eph.4:15)	v. and of the **knowledge of the Son of God,**
	vi. to be a **perfect man,**
	vii. to the measure of the stature of the *fullness of Christ*; (Eph.4:11-13)
	viii. **You will grow** to become in **every respect the mature body of Him** who is the head, that is, Christ. (Eph.4:15/NIV)
	ix. **From Christ,** the whole body, joined and held together by every supporting ligament, **grows and builds itself up in love,** as each part does its work. (Eph.4:16/NIV)

PART III

Commandments Of God From
The Book Of Philippians

Book of Philippians

Paul, an apostle of Jesus Christ, wrote this epistle to the *Philippian believers* in the year A.D. 62/63 during his *prolonged imprisonment,* most likely in Rome.

The church in Philippi was established by Paul and his co-laborers, Silas, Timothy and Luke, during his *second missionary journey.* This was a generous church which supported Paul financially. (Acts 16; Phil.4:15-16)

The main theme of this letter is *"Joy in living for Christ"* and it focuses on Christ Jesus as the purpose for living.

"Put it into practice—whatever you have learned or received or heard from me, or seen in me," says Apostle Paul. (Phil. 4:9/NIV)

1. Be Worthy Of The Gospel When You Suffer For Christ

COMMANDMENTS OF GOD FOR US TO OBEY	REWARDS FOR OBEDIENCE/ CONSEQUENCES OF DISOBEDIENCE/ SUPPORTING SCRIPTURES
1. Whatever happens, conduct yourselves in a manner *worthy of the Gospel* of Christ.—Apostle Paul. (Phil. 1:27/NIV) 2. *Stand fast in one spirit*, with one mind striving together for the faith of the gospel.—Apostle Paul. (Phil. 1:27) 3. Do *not be frightened* in any way by those who oppose you.— Apostle Paul. (Phil. 1:28/NIV)	i. Then it is a sign to those who oppose you that *they will be destroyed,* but that *you will be saved—and that by God.* (Phil. 1:28/NIV) ii. For it has been granted to you on behalf of Christ not only to believe on Him, but also to *suffer for Him,* as Apostle Paul did. (Phil.1:29/NIV) iii. *He who has begun a good work in you will complete it* until the day of Jesus Christ.—Apostle Paul. (Phil.1:6)

Points to Ponder!

- *If we suffer, we shall also reign with Him...*Be encouraged that in the end, the wicked will be destroyed in hell-fire and the righteous will be saved for eternity. (2 Tim.2:12)

- *Epaphroditus held in high esteem for his suffering for Christ...* Apostle Paul sent Epaphroditus, his fellow worker and fellow soldier in Christ, to the church of Philippi, requesting them to receive him in the Lord with all gladness, and *hold such men in esteem.*

- *For the work of Christ, Epaphroditus came close to death,* not regarding his life, to minister to Paul's need which the Philippian church failed to do for Paul. (Phil.2:25-30)

2. Count All Things Loss To Gain Christ

COMMANDMENTS OF GOD FOR US TO OBEY	REWARDS FOR OBEDIENCE/ SUPPORTING SCRIPTURES
1. Whatever things that are gain to you, count these loss for Christ, as Apostle Paul did. (Phil.3:7) 2. Count all things loss and rubbish, *for the excellence of the knowledge of Christ Jesus*, your Lord, as Apostle Paul did. (Phil.3:8)	*So that...* i. You may **gain Christ** and be found in Him. (Phil.3:8-9/NIV) ii. You may not have your own righteousness that comes from the law. (Phil.3:9/NIV) iii. But you may have the **righteousness which is through faith in Christ**—the righteousness that comes from God on the basis of faith.—Apostle Paul. (Phil.3:9/NIV

Pause & Think!

What profit is it to a man *if he gains the whole world, and loses his own soul?* (Matt.16:26)

3. Destruction For The Enemies Of The Cross Of Christ

COMMANDMENTS OF GOD FOR US TO OBEY	REWARDS FOR OBEDIENCE/ CONSEQUENCES OF DISOBEDIENCE
1. Do not live as enemies of the Cross of Christ.—Apostle Paul. (Phil.3:18/NIV) 2. *"Join together in following my example,* brethren."—Apostle Paul. (Phil.3:17/NIV)	i. For their *destiny is destruction.* ii. Their *god is their stomach.* iii. Their glory is in their shame. iv. Their *mind is set on earthly things.* (Phil.3:19/NIV) v. But *our citizenship is in Heaven.*—Apostle Paul. (Phil.3:20)

Pause & Think!

Apostle Paul states, "Imitate me, just as I also imitate Christ." (1 Cor.11:1)

Here, Apostle Paul asks us to follow his example because he never boasted about anything else but the cross of Christ. (1 Cor.11:1)

4. Eagerly Wait For The Savior, The Lord Jesus Christ

COMMANDMENTS OF GOD FOR US TO OBEY	REWARDS FOR OBEDIENCE/ SUPPORTING SCRIPTURES
1. Eagerly wait for the Savior, the Lord Jesus Christ. (Phil.3:20)	i. For *our citizenship is in Heaven.* (Phil.3:20) ii. For Lord Jesus Christ, by the power that enables Him to bring everything under His control, will *transform our lowly bodies* so that they will *be like His glorious body.* (Phil.3:21/NIV)
2. Stand fast in the Lord. (Phil.4:1) 3. Let your *gentleness* be known to all men. (Phil. 4:5)	For the Lord is at hand. (Phil.4:5)

4.1. Lord Jesus Christ, The King Of Kings Is Coming Soon!

I. Two Events Of The Second Coming Of Christ

- Rapture or The Secret Coming of Christ
- The Visible Second Coming of Christ

Secret Coming of Christ—Rapture	Visible Second Coming of Christ
What is Rapture?	
1. In Christian eschatology, the Rapture is a reference to *"being caught up."* (1 Thess.4:14-17) 2. The Rapture is *for the ready Church,* the Body of Christ. (1Thess.4-5; 1 Cor.15:50-54) 3. Only those who anticipate Christ's secret coming *will see Him* and will be taken up to Heaven. (Rev 3:10; Mat 5:8; Heb. 9:28)	i. In the Second coming of Christ, *everyone, including those who pierced Him, will see Him.* (Zech.12:10; Rev 1:7) ii. Jesus Christ will come down from Heaven *with His Saints after the tribulation period.* (Zech. 14:5; Col. 3:4; Matt 24:29-31)

Where is the promise of His coming?

Apostle Peter says, "Scoffers will come in the last days, walking according to their own lusts, and saying, *"Where is the promise of His coming?*

For since the fathers fell asleep, *all things continue as they were from the beginning of creation."* (2 Pet.3:3-4)

But, beloved, *The Lord is not slack* concerning *His* promise, as some count slackness, but is *patient with you, not willing that any should perish* but that all should come to repentance. (2 Pet.3:9)

Be Warned!

II. *Purpose Of Christ's Coming*

Secret Coming of Christ—Rapture	Visible Second Coming of Christ
1. **To Rescue the Church from the Wrath of God**...The Rapture is to save the Church, the Body of Christ from the wrath of God which will be poured on the earth during the great tribulation of anti-christ. (Lk.21:36; Rev.3:10)	1. Jesus comes for the Jews and Gentiles who are **redeemed** during tribulation. (Zech 14:1-3) 2. Christ will **execute judgment** on all people. (Rev. 19:11-21; Jude 1:14-15) 3. The Lord of lords will then **set up His 1000 year Millennial Kingdom** on earth. (Rev. 20:4-6)
Satan cast down from Heaven to earth... 2. **War will break out in Heaven.** Michael and his angels will fight with the dragon and his fallen angels. The heavenly hosts will prevail over satan and his fallen angels. (Rev. 12:7-8) 3. **Satan,** the great dragon, who deceives the whole world, along with his fallen angels, will be **cast out of Heaven to the earth.** (Rev. 12:9) 4. **Woe to the inhabitants of the earth** and the sea! For Satan, the accuser of brethren, who **accuses us before our God day and night,** comes down to the earth, having **great wrath,** because he knows that he has a short time. (Rev. 12:10-12) 5. Satan, in his fury, **sends the man of sin, the antichrist,** to torment people on the earth during the great tribulation period. (2 Thess. 2:3-12)	*Satan cast into the bottomless pit...* 4. Jesus sends His angel to cast the dragon, that serpent of old who is the Devil and Satan, into the bottomless pit, and shut him up, and set a seal on him so that he should **deceive the nations no more** till the 1000 years are finished. (Rev 20:1-3)

| 6. *Believers who stand firm for Christ will overcome Satan* by the *blood of the Lamb*, and by the *word of their testimony*; and they will *not love their lives unto death*. (Rev.12:10-11)

7. Please note that there are *4 theological opinions* about rapture:

- Pre-Tribulation Rapture
- Mid-Tribulation Rapture
- Post-Tribulation Rapture
- No Rapture – only Second Coming of Christ	

III. *Supernatural Occurrences During Rapture & Second Coming Of Christ*

Secret Coming of Christ—Rapture	Visible Second Coming of Christ
Be Prepared To Meet The Lord Jesus In The Air... *Comfort one another with these words...* Apostle Paul says, by the Word of the Lord, that... 1. *The Lord Himself will descend from heaven* with a shout, with the voice of an archangel, and with the *trumpet of God*. (1 Thess.4:14) 2. And the *dead in Christ will rise first*. (1 Thess.4:16)	*Jesus' feet on the earth...* 1. In that day, the Lord Jesus will come down to the earth and *His feet will stand on the Mount of Olives*, which faces Jerusalem on the east. (Zech.14:4) 2. The *Mount of Olives shall be* **split in two,** from east to west. (Zech.14:4) 3. *Jesus coming with His army, the Saints...*The Lord, our God will come on a white horse with all His saints, including those who are caught up in rapture. The saints will be clothed in fine linen, white and clean. (Zech.14:5; Rev.19:14)

Secret Coming of Christ—Rapture	Visible Second Coming of Christ
3. Then we who are alive *and* remain shall be *caught up together* with them in the clouds to meet the Lord *in the air.* And thus we shall always be with the Lord. (1 Thess.4:17)	4. *Angels gather the elect…*He will send His angels with a great sound of a trumpet, and they will gather together His elect from the four winds, from one end of heaven to the other. (Matt.24:31)
4. Behold, I tell you a mystery: We shall *not all sleep,* but *we shall all be changed—in a moment,* in the twinkling of an eye, *at the last trumpet.* (1 Cor.15:50-53)	5. *Armegaddon War…*The Faithful and True God, the Righteous Judge will make war against the nations of the world in the Battle of Armegaddon. (Rev.19:11, 15)
Then "Death is swallowed up in victory." (1 Cor.15:54)	6. *War against the Almighty God…* The King of kings, Jesus Christ, with a sharp sword that goes out of His mouth, smites the beast, the kings of the earth and their armies who will be gathered together *to make war against Him.* (Rev.19:15,19)
	7. *Judgment on the Anti-christ…* The beast i.e., the anti-christ and the false prophet, who deceive the people on earth to receive the mark of the beast, will be taken and *cast alive into a lake of fire* burning with brimstone. (Rev 19:19-20; Jude 1:14,15)
	8. *Victorious Christ…*Thus the fierce wrath of Almighty God will be poured upon His enemies, the beast, the kings of the earth and their armies. (Rev.19:15-21; Jude 1:14-15)

IV. *Timing Of The Second Coming Of Christ*

Secret Coming of Christ—Rapture	Visible Second Coming of Christ
The day and hour unknown...	*Is Jesus Your Savior or Your Judge?*
1. "That day and hour no one knows, not even the angels of heaven, but My Father only," says Jesus. (Matt.24:36)	1. *As the lightning* comes from the east and flashes to the west, so also will the coming of the Son of Man be. (Matt.24:27)
2. You be ready, for the Son of Man is coming at an hour you do not expect *as a thief in the night*. (Matt.24:42-44)	2. Take heed to yourselves, lest your hearts be weighed down with carousing, drunkenness, and cares of this life and that Day come on you *unexpectedly*. (Lk.21:34)
	3. For it will come *as a snare* on all those who dwell on the face of the whole earth.(Lk.21:35)
Make sure you are not left behind...	4. *Immediately after the tribulation of those days...*
3. Two *men* will be in the field: one will be taken and the other left. (Matt.24:40)	i. the sun will be darkened,
Two *women will be* grinding at the mill: one will be taken and the other left. (Matt.24:41)	ii. the moon will not give its light;
	iii. the stars will fall from heaven,
4. Watch therefore, for you do not know what hour your Lord is coming. (Matt.24:42)	iv. the powers of the heavens will be shaken. (Matt.24:29)
	Then the sign of the Son of Man will appear in heaven.
5. All the prophecies concerning the second coming of Christ are already fulfilled. So rapture can happen any day at any moment.	Then *all the tribes of the earth will mourn.*
	5. They will *see the Son of Man* coming on the clouds of heaven *with power and great glory*. (Matt.24:30)

V. Be Rapture Ready...Watch & Pray

Watch & Pray... Now that you know rapture is definitely going to happen, watch and pray and prepare yourselves and your loved ones to meet the Lord in the air. (Matt.24:42)

*Stand in the Gap...*Since rapture is imminent, **cry out to God for the salvation of your unsaved** relatives, friends, neighbors, colleagues and people living in your streets, city and nation.

Salvation is the best gift you can give to your fellow human beings in these last days. Give them their **Messiah, Jesus Christ!**

*Prophecies already fulfilled...*All the prophecies concerning the second coming of Christ are already fulfilled. So rapture can happen any day at any moment.

*Escape the great tribulation...*Watch therefore, and pray always that you may be counted worthy to escape all these things that will come to pass during the great tribulation period of antichrist, and to stand before the Son of Man. (Lk.21:36)

VI. Do Not Be Deceived By Antichrist, The Beast

*   *Antichrist to be revealed soon...*The Day of the Lord, the visible Second Coming of Christ will not come until the antichrist, the **man of sin** is revealed first. (2 Thess.2:3)

*   *World stage set for the Antichrist...*The mystery of lawlessness, the antichrist is already at work. (2 Thess.2:7)

*   *Antichrist opposes God...*Antichrist, the **son of perdition**, will oppose and exalt himself above God. (2 Thess.2:4)

*   *Antichrist sits in the Temple of God...*The **abomination of desolation**, the antichrist will sit as God in the third temple which is soon to be rebuilt in Israel. (2 Thess.2:4; Dan.9:27)

- *Antichrist calls himself "God"…*He will show himself that he is God. (2 Thess.2:4; Dan.9:27)

- *Satan empowers Antichrist…*The coming of the lawless one is according to the *working of Satan, with all power, signs, and lying wonders.* (2 Thess.2:9)

- *Perishing souls will be deceived…*The antichrist will come with *all unrighteous deception* among those who perish, because *they did not receive the love of the truth, that they might be saved.* (2 Thess.2:10)

- *Condemned for not receiving Jesus, the Truth…*For this reason God will send them *strong delusion* that they should *believe the lie of the antichrist* that they all may be condemned who did not believe the truth but *had pleasure in unrighteousness.* (2 Thess.2:11-12)

- *Judgment on the Antichrist, the Beast…*The Lord will consume the antichrist with the breath of His mouth and *destroy him* with the brightness of His coming. (2 Thess.2:8)

VII. *Do Not Receive The Mark Or The Name of the Beast Or The Number of His Name*

- *2000 Year Old Bible Prophecy:* "He causes all, both small and great, rich and poor, free and bond, to receive a mark in their *right hand, or in their foreheads*: (Rev. 13:16)

- *No man might buy or sell, save he that had the mark*, or the name of the beast, or the number of his name." (Rev. 13:17)

- *Fulfillment of Bible Prophecy:* Approximately 2000 years later, the microchip technology is available right now for this prophecy to be fulfilled in our generation. Be warned!

VIII. *Eternal Torment For Those Who Receive The Mark Of The Beast*

"If anyone worships the beast and his image, and receives his mark on his forehead or on his hand...(Rev.14:9)

- He himself shall also **drink of the wine of the wrath of God,** which is poured out full strength into the cup of His indignation. (Rev.14:10)

- He shall be **tormented with fire and brimstone** in the presence of the holy angels and in the presence of the Lamb of God, Jesus Christ. (Rev.14:10)

- The **smoke of their torment ascends forever and ever.** (Rev.14:11)

- They have **no rest day or night,** who worship the beast and his image, and whoever receives the mark of his name."(Rev.14:11)

5. God Will Supply All Your Needs When You Help The Servants of God

COMMANDMENTS OF GOD FOR US TO OBEY	REWARDS FOR OBEDIENCE/ SUPPORTING SCRIPTURES
1. Share in the distress of the Servants of God, as the Philippian church did to Apostle Paul. (Phil.4:14) 2. Share with the Servants of God concerning giving and receiving, as the Philippian church did to Apostle Paul. (Phil.4:15)	*So that...* i. The *fruit will abound to your account.* (Phil.4:17) ii. It will be *a sweet-smelling aroma, an acceptable sacrifice, well pleasing to God.* (Phil.4:18) iii. *God shall supply all your need* according to His riches in glory by Christ Jesus.—Apostle Paul. (Phil.4:19)

*Greet one another...*We should greet every saint in Christ Jesus, as Apostle Paul exhorts the Philippian Church to do. (Phil.4:21)

6. In Christ, You Are Circumcised In The Heart

COMMANDMENTS OF GOD FOR US TO OBEY	REWARDS FOR OBEDIENCE/ SUPPORTING SCRIPTURES
1. Watch out for the dogs, those evildoers, those mutilators of the flesh (circumcision). (Phil. 3:2/NIV) 2. Boast in Christ Jesus, as Apostle Paul did. (Phil.3:3/NIV) 3. Have no confidence in the flesh.—Apostle Paul. (Phil 3:4)	*Boast in Christ Jesus*...For we are the circumcision (of the heart) who serve God by His Spirit. (Phil. 3:3/NIV)

Points to Ponder...

- *Circumcised in the heart*...Apostle Paul states that we, gentile believers need not be circumcised in the flesh like the Jews, for we are circumcised in the heart, as believers in Christ.

- Paul calls those who impose circumcision upon the gentile believers as *"dogs and mutilators of the flesh."*

- The Lord Jesus says that we should *not put heavy yoke* on people, as the teachers of the law did.

- *Rejoice...*Paul exhorts us to rejoice, for in Christ we are set free from all the rituals and traditions (e.g., circumcision) imposed by religion. (Phil.3:3)

7. Jesus—The Name Above Every Name

COMMANDMENTS OF GOD FOR US TO OBEY	REWARDS FOR OBEDIENCE/ SUPPORTING SCRIPTURES
1. *At the Name of Jesus...* *Every knee should bow* of those in heaven, and of those on earth, and of those under the earth. 2. Every tongue should confess that Jesus Christ is Lord, to the glory of God the Father. (Phil.2:10-11)	i. For God has *highly exalted* Christ Jesus, and given Him the Name which is above every name. (Phil.2:9) ii. Salvation is found in no one else, for there is *no other name under heaven but the Name of Jesus*, given among men by which we must be saved. (Acts 4:12/NIV)

I. *Jesus' Name, far above every name that is named...*

1. God raised Christ from the dead with the incomparable great power of the Holy Spirit;

2. God seated Christ at His right hand in the heavenly realms,

3. *far above all rule, and authority, and power, and dominion,*

4. *far above every name that is named,*

5. not only in this world, but also in that which is to come;

6. *God has put all things under Christ's feet;*

7. God appointed *Christ to be Head* over everything for the church, which is His body.

8. The *fullness of Christ fills all in all.* (Eph.1:19-23)

II. *When you put Jesus first, above everything else in your life, & Obey His Commandments...*

- *Blessings* of God will overtake you. (Matt.6:33; Deut.28:2)

- *Goodness and mercy* of God will follow you all the days of your life. God's *favor* will surround you as a shield. (Ps.23:6; 5:12)

- Blessed are those who do His Commandments that they may have the right to the *tree of life*, and may enter through the gates into the city. (Rev.22:14)

7.1. The Awesome Name of Jesus!

I. Salvation In The Name of Jesus!

- *Salvation in Jesus' Name...* Salvation is found in no one else, for **there is no other name under heaven but the Name of Jesus given to mankind by which we must be saved**. (Acts. 4:10,12/NIV)

- *Receive Forgiveness & the Gift of the Holy Spirit in Jesus' Name...* "Repent, and be baptized every one of you **in the Name of Jesus Christ** for the forgiveness of your sins. And you will receive the gift of the Holy Spirit," said Peter to the multitudes. (Acts 2:38/NIV)

II. Eternal Life In The Name of Jesus!

- *Eternal Life in Jesus' Name...*Many signs are written in the Scriptures so that you may believe that *Jesus is the Messiah*, the Son of God, and that by believing you may have *life in His Name*. (Jn.20:30-31/NIV)

III. Power In The Name of Jesus!

- *Holy Spirit, the Helper sent by Father God in Jesus' Name...* "The Helper, the Holy Spirit, whom the Father will send in My Name, He will **teach you all things**, and bring to your remembrance all things that I said to you." (Jn.14:26)

- *Do Signs & Wonders in Jesus' Name...* Jesus declared, "These signs will follow those who believe:

In My Name...

they will cast out demons;

they will speak with new tongues;

they will take up serpents;

and if they drink anything deadly, it will by no means hurt them; they will lay hands on the sick, and they will recover." (Mk.16:17-18)

- *Work Miracles in Jesus' Name...* John said to Jesus, "Teacher, we saw someone, who does not follow us, casting out demons in Your Name, and we forbade him because he does not follow us."

But Jesus said, "Do not forbid him, for no one who **works a miracle in My Name** can soon afterward speak evil of Me. For he, who is not against us, is on our side. (Mk.9:38-40)

IV. *Ask & Receive In The Name of Jesus!*

- *Pray together in Jesus' Name...*"Where two or three are gathered together in My Name, **I am there in the midst** of them," promises the Lord Jesus Christ. (Matt.18:20)

- *Ask & Receive in Jesus' Name...*The Lord Jesus says to those who believe in Him, "Whatever you ask in My Name, that **I will do**, that the Father may be glorified in the Son. (Jn.14:13)

- *Ask Anything in Jesus' Name...*If you ask anything in My Name, **I will do it**. (Jn.14:14)

- *Ask the Father in Jesus' Name...*Jesus said to His disciples, "Most assuredly, I say to you, whatever you ask the Father in My Name **He will give you**." (Jn.16:23)

- *Ask in Jesus' Name & Receive that your Joy may be full...*"Until now you have asked nothing in My Name. Ask, and you will receive, that your joy may be full." (Jn.16:24)

V. *Be Great In The Name of Jesus!*

- *Receive a little Child in Jesus' Name...* Jesus said, "Whoever receives a little child in My Name **receives Me**; and whoever receives Me **receives Him who sent Me**. For he who is **least among you all will be great**." (Lk.9:48)

VI. *Do Good Deeds & Get Rewards In The Name of Jesus!*

- *Bless the Children of God in Jesus' Name...*Jesus said, "Whoever gives you a cup of water to drink in My Name, because you belong to

Christ, assuredly, I say to you, *he will by no means lose his reward."* (Mk.9:41)

- **Do Every Good Thing in Jesus' Name...**Whatever you do, in word or deed, do everything in the Name of the Lord Jesus, giving thanks to God the Father through Him. (Col. 3:17)

VII. *Surrender At The Name of Jesus!*

- **Every knee should bow at the Name of Jesus...**God exalted Jesus to the highest place and gave Him the Name that is above every name, that at the Name of Jesus every knee should bow, in heaven and on earth and under the earth, and every tongue confess that Jesus Christ is Lord, to the glory of God the Father. (Phil.2:9-11/NIV)

Jesus' Name Truly Has Power!

8. Let The Mind Of Christ Be In You

If you have any encouragement from being *united with Christ,*
if any comfort from His love,
if any *fellowship with the Spirit,*
if any tenderness and compassion, *then you will have the mind of Christ,*
says Apostle Paul. (Phil.2:1/NIV)

COMMANDMENTS OF GOD FOR US TO OBEY	REWARDS FOR OBEDIENCE/ SUPPORTING SCRIPTURES
To Receive the Mind of Christ...	*What is the Mind of Christ?*
1. Be like minded, have the same love and be one in spirit and purpose. (Phil.2:2/NIV)	i. Jesus Christ, being in the **form of God**, did **not** consider it robbery to be **equal with God.** (Phil.2:6)
2. Do nothing out of selfish ambition or vain conceit. (Phil.2:3/NIV)	ii. But Christ made Himself of **no reputation.** (Phil.2:7)
3. In humility, consider others better than yourselves. (Phil.2:3/NIV)	iii. Christ took the form of a **bondservant.** (Phil.2:7)
4. Each of you should look, not only to your own interests but also to the interests of others. (Phil.2:4/NIV)	iv. Christ came in the **likeness of men.** (Phil.2:7)
	v. Jesus **humbled** Himself, being found in appearance as a Man. (Phil.2:8)
5. Let this mind be in you which was also in Christ Jesus. (Phil.2:5)	vi. Jesus became **obedient to the point of death,** even the death of the cross. (Phil.2:8)
	Therefore, God also has **highly exalted** Him and given Him the name which is above every name. (Phil.2:9)

Points to Ponder... As God highly exalted Jesus Christ, you too will be exalted when you have the mind of Christ.

Apostle Paul commends Timothy for having the mind of Christ... Apostle Paul says that he found no one *like-minded* as Timothy who *sincerely cared for other believers.* For all seek their own, not the things which are of Christ Jesus. (Phil.2:2-5, 19-23)

9. Let The Peace Of God Guard Your Hearts & Minds

COMMANDMENTS OF GOD FOR US TO OBEY	REWARDS FOR OBEDIENCE/ SUPPORTING SCRIPTURES
1. *Do not be anxious* about anything. (Phil.4:6/NIV) 2. In everything, by *prayer* and petition, *with thanksgiving,* present your requests to God. (Phil.4:6/NIV)	And the *peace of God,* which transcends all understanding will guard your hearts and your minds in Christ Jesus. (Phil.4:7/NIV)
Fill your mind with good things... 3. Brothers, Whatever is *true,* Whatever is noble, Whatever is right, Whatever is *pure,* Whatever is lovely, Whatever is admirable, If anything is excellent or praiseworthy *Think about such things.* (Phil.4:8/NIV) 4. *Put it into practice*—whatever you have *learned, or received or heard from me, or seen in me,* says apostle Paul. (Phil.4:9/NIV)	And the *God of Peace will be with you.* (Phil.4:9/NIV)

10. Preach Christ Out Of Love & Defend The Gospel

COMMANDMENTS OF GOD FOR US TO OBEY	REWARDS FOR OBEDIENCE/ SUPPORTING SCRIPTURES
1. Do not preach Christ out of envy and rivalry but preach Christ out of goodwill. (Phil.1:15/NIV) 2. Preach Christ out of love and defend the gospel, as Apostle Paul did. (Phil.1:16/NIV) 3. Do not preach Christ out of selfish ambition but preach Christ sincerely. (Phil.1:17/NIV)	The important thing is that in every way, whether from false motives or true, Christ is preached. (Phil.1:18/NIV)

❖ To be an efficient *Soul Winner*, every Servant of God should fervently *pray for the following*:

i. Burden for Souls. (Ps.2:8; Ezek.22:30)

ii. Gift of Faith. (1Cor.12:9)

iii. Signs & Wonders in Ministry. (Mk.16:17-18)

iv. Visions & Dreams from God. (Joel 2:28; Jer.33:3)

v. To see Jesus, to hear His voice daily and to know His will. (Acts 22:14; Jn.10:16)

vi. 9 Gifts of the Holy Spirit. (1 Cor.12:1-11)

vii. 9 Fruits of the Holy Spirit. (Gal.5:22)

viii. Anointing to cast out Demons. (Lk.10:19; Mk.16:17)

ix. Boldness to Witness for Christ. (Acts 4:29)

x. Fire of the Holy Spirit. (Lk.3:16)

xi. Great Joy to serve God. (Phil.4:4)

xii. Favor & Mercy of God. (Prov.3:1-4; Heb.4:16)

11. Press Towards The Call Of God In Christ

COMMANDMENTS OF GOD FOR US TO OBEY	REWARDS FOR OBEDIENCE/ SUPPORTING SCRIPTURES
1. **Press on** to take hold of that for which Christ Jesus took hold of you.—Apostle Paul. (Phil.3:12/NIV) 2. **Forget those things which are behind** and reach forward to those things which are ahead.—Apostle Paul. (Phil.3:13) 3. **Press toward the goal for the prize** of the upward call of God in Christ Jesus.—Apostle Paul. (Phil.3:14) 4. Let us, **as many as are mature,** have this mind. (Phil.3:15) 5. Let us walk by the same rule, let us be of the **same mind,** as Apostle Paul had. (Phil.3:16)	*So that...* i. You may **know Christ**. (Phil.3:10) ii. You may **know the power** of His resurrection. (Phil.3:10) iii. You may **know the fellowship of His sufferings.** (Phil.3:10) iv. You may **become like Him** in His death. (Phil.3:10/NIV) v. You may attain to the **resurrection** from the dead.—Apostle Paul. (Phil.3:11)
6. "**Join together in following my example,** brethren." — Apostle Paul. (Phil.3:17/NIV) 7. "Keep your eyes on those who live as we do," says apostle Paul. (Phil.3:17/NIV)	i. For many **live as enemies of the cross of Christ**. (Phil.3:18/NIV) ii. For their **destiny is destruction**. (Phil.3:19/NIV) iii. But **our citizenship is in Heaven.**—Apostle Paul. (Phil.3:20)

12. Rejoice In The Lord, For Your Names Are In The Book Of Life!

COMMANDMENTS OF GOD FOR US TO OBEY	REWARDS FOR OBEDIENCE/ SUPPORTING SCRIPTURES
1. Rejoice in the Lord, my brethren. (Phil. 3:1) 2. Rejoice in the Lord always. Again I say, rejoice.—Apostle Paul. (Phil. 4:4)	For the Lord is at hand. (Phil. 4:5)
3. "Rejoice," says Lord Jesus. (Lk.10:20)	For *your names are written in Heaven*. (Lk.10:20)
4. Let us be glad and rejoice and give Him glory. (Rev.19:7)	For the *marriage of the Lamb* has come, and *His wife has made herself ready*. (Rev.19:7)

Pause & Think!

- *Rejoice in the Lord*, O you righteous! For praise from the upright is beautiful. (Ps.33:1)

- My soul will *rejoice* in the Lord and delight in His *Salvation*. (Ps.35:9)

- The righteous will *rejoice* in the Lord and take refuge in Him. (Ps.64:10)

- Sing to God, sing praises to His name, extol Him who rides on the clouds; *rejoice* before Him – *His name is the Lord*. (Ps.68:4)

- In Your presence is *fullness of joy*; at Your right hand are pleasures forever more. (Ps.16:11)

12.1. Rejoice, You are Invited To The Marriage Of The Lamb!

- Scripture gives another reason for us to rejoice and be glad; for the marriage of the Lamb is at hand. And **"Blessed are they which are called *unto the marriage* supper of the Lamb."** (Rev.19:6-9)

- *The righteous church, His Bride...*The church, His bride must be ready to be taken to Heaven in rapture to meet her Bridegroom, Jesus Christ.

- *Price to pay to be the Bride of Christ...*The bride should be arrayed in fine linen, clean and white; for the fine linen is the righteousness of saints. (Rev.19:8)

- *Are you willing to pay the price to be the Bride?* Every believer is called to be the Bride of Christ. The bride should be pure, holy, righteous, without any blemish and delivered from all impurity.

- *Are you the Bride of Christ or the Guest at the marriage of the Lamb?* The Lord says that blessed are those who are called as guests at the marriage supper of the Lamb. (Rev.19:9)

- How much more blessed will be the Bride of Jesus Christ at the marriage of the Lamb?

- *Reward...*To be the Bride of Christ is the most honorable reward a believer can receive in Heaven. (Hos.2:19-20; 2 Cor.11:2)

13. Work Out Your Own Salvation With Fear & Trembling

Salvation is a free gift of God by grace through faith in Jesus Christ. But after you are saved, you are expected to work out your own Salvation by living your life in the reverential fear of God. (Rom.10:9; Phil.2:12)

COMMANDMENTS OF GOD FOR US TO OBEY	REWARDS FOR OBEDIENCE/ SUPPORTING SCRIPTURES
1. Work out your own salvation with fear and trembling. (Phil.2:12)	For it is *God who works in you* both to will and to do *for His good pleasure.*(Phil.2:13)
How Do You Work Out Your Own Salvation? 2. Do all things without murmuring and disputing. (Phil.2:14) 3. *Hold fast the Word of Life.* (Phil.2:16)	i. So that you may become *blameless* and *pure,* "children of God *without fault* in a crooked and depraved generation." (Phil.2:15) ii. For in the midst of a perverse generation, you *shine as lights in the world.* (Phil.2:15)

Work Out Your Own Salvation – By Obeying God's Commandments

o   The Lord says, *"If you love Me, obey My commandments."* We express our love for Jesus through our obedience. (Jn.14:15)

o   *The Key...*Our obedience to God is directly proportionate to our love for Him. For example, if you *obey 40% of Jesus' commandments*, it may mean, *you love Christ only 40%.*

o   If you obey 90% of Jesus' commandments, it may mean, you love Christ 90%. Still you leave 10% loophole to Satan, for the Devil to backstab you. Hence, it is better to obey the Lord 100%. Obedience is the foundational key for your intimacy with Jesus.

13.1. Jesus, Tempted Just Like Us, Yet Without Sin

*Only those who endure till the end shall be saved...*Though Salvation is the free gift of God to mankind through Christ Jesus, Scripture says that only those who endure till the end shall be saved. (*Eternal Salvation*) Hence once you accept Jesus Christ as your Savior, for the rest of your life, you need to work out your own salvation by resisting sin with the help of the Holy Spirit. (Matt.24:13; Rom.10:9-10; Phil.2:12; Jude 1:3; Heb.5:9; 9:28)

*You are being saved all your life...*For the message of the cross is foolishness to those who are perishing, but to us who are *being saved* it is the power of God. (1 Cor.1:18)

*Jesus, tempted just like us...*Jesus, when He walked on this earth in the flesh, was tempted in every way, just like we are, yet He did not sin. (Heb.4:15)

Jesus learnt obedience through suffering, by denying His fleshly desires... Jesus, as a human being, went through suffering to resist all the temptations of the flesh in order to learn obedience. (Heb.5:8)

*Jesus, our High Priest, empathizes with our weaknesses...*We do not have a high priest who is unable to empathize with our weaknesses, but we have one who has been tempted in every way, just as we are—yet he did not sin. (Heb. 4:14-15)

*Grace of God available to help us overcome sin...*Let us then approach God's throne of grace with confidence, so that we may receive mercy and find grace to help us in our time of need. (Heb. 4:16)

14. You Can Do All Things Through Christ Jesus

COMMANDMENTS OF GOD FOR US TO OBEY	REWARDS FOR OBEDIENCE
1. Be content whatever the circumstances, as Apostle Paul was. (Phil.4:11/NIV)	For Christ *Jesus will strengthen you* as He strengthened Apostle Paul. (Phil.4:13)
2. *Learn the secret of being content* in any and every situation, whether well fed or hungry, whether living in plenty or in want, as apostle Paul did. (Phil.4:11-12/NIV)	
3. Do all things through Christ Jesus, as Apostle Paul did. (Phil.4:13)	

Pause & Think!

- *Find out the secret…*Apostle Paul learnt the secret that he could do all things through Jesus Christ who strengthened him.

- *You can do whatever you are called to do…*Christ's power and grace enables us to do everything that He has called us to do and also to be content in every situation.

- Jesus Himself says, *"Without Me you can do nothing."* (Jn.15:5)

14.1. You Can Do Greater Things Than What Jesus Did

*God molds your character before using you mightily....*When you are called by God to fulfill a greater purpose for His Kingdom, God will first take you through *His School of Training* to mold your character *into His image*. Your *"Ego, Self & I"* must die. It is a process and it depends on how quickly you yield to the Holy Spirit. The vessel has to be prepared so that he can do greater things than Jesus Himself.

*God trains you to Die to Self...*One of the ways to die to self is this—*God will put people with different attitudes in your path* to mold your character and to prepare you to do greater works for Him.

If you cannot *overcome the deeds of your flesh* like anger, pride, unforgiveness, bitterness, selfishness, lack of love, lust, etc., you cannot fulfill 100% of God's will for your life. God cannot use you mightily until you fully surrender to the leading of the Holy Spirit.

Total surrender to God = Pain of dying to Self + 100% Obedience to God

1. Ways to Die to Self

Some of the ways by which the Holy Spirit helps you crucify your flesh...

- *By Meditating "The Word"...*You should meditate on the Word of God *day and night* and the *Word of God will purify you*. (Ps.1:2; 105:19; Josh.1:8)

- *By Hearing Audio Bible...*You can hear the Word of God on Bible audio tapes and fill your mind with things of above, thereby *renewing your mind*. (Phil.4:8)

- *By Praying without ceasing...*You should come to the level of praying without ceasing. Then dying to self will be easy. (1 Thes.5:17)

- *By Praying in the Spirit 15-30 minutes daily...*You can pray in the gift of tongues at least for 15-30 minutes everyday which is the *shortcut to your calling*.

- *By the Anointing of the Holy Spirit...*You must daily wait on the Holy Spirit until He *cleanses your temple* for Him to dwell in and *strengthen your inner man* to overcome any temptation that the devil puts in your path.

- *By the Power of the Holy Spirit...*The Holy Spirit *removes the root of the lust of the flesh* from deep within your heart.—*Author's Experience*

Moses, an Extra-Ordinary Leader

2. Outward Signs of Dying to Self

*The prepared vessel bears the fruit of the Holy Spirit...*Once you are trained by God, you will have the fruit of the Holy Spirit and you will be able to *overcome your attitude problems, the lust of the flesh, etc. which may hinder your calling.* Then you can handle any personality and adjust with any human being, to achieve the greater vision that God has conceived in your heart.

3. Lessons to learn from the Biblical Characters...

I. Moses had to first "Die to Self" to become an Extra-ordinary Leader

*i. Moses, a Prepared Vessel...*Moses was prepared by the Lord for 80 years to deliver 2 million Israelites from slavery in Egypt. God molded his character and trained him for 40 years as a prince in the palace and 40 years in the wilderness as a shepherd. *It took Moses 80 years to die to Self, I, ego, etc.* (Ex.2-3)

*ii. Moses lost his temper...*Moses became the meekest man on earth and yet when the Israelites provoked him in the wilderness and murmured against him for lack of water, he could not control his anger. Instead of speaking to the rock as the Lord had instructed him to bring water out of the rock, he struck the rock twice with his rod in anger. (Num. 20:7-11)

iii. Moses' Disobedience prevented him from Fulfilling his Calling to the end... For whatever Moses did was symbolic of what was to happen in Christ's life. In the New Testament, the rock which Moses struck represents Jesus Christ, the spring of Living Water. (1 Cor.10:4)

Christ was to be Crucified only once for our Redemption, as Moses was commanded by God to strike the rock in the first instance of bringing water out of the rock. In the second incident, Moses struck the rock twice in anger when God had asked him to just speak to the rock. This is symbolic of Christ being crucified twice. Therefore God could not forgive

Moses but punished him for his short temper and disobedience to God's command and did not let Moses lead the Israelites into the promised land, which was his ultimate calling. (Ex.17:1-7; Num.20:1-13; Is.53)

iv. Moses' one act of Disobedience cost him Entry into the Promised Land...
God's purpose in preparing Moses for 80 years was for him to lead the Israelites into the promised land. Sadly, Moses died in the desert without entering the promised land due to his disobedience. But God was so pleased with Moses' extra-ordinary leadership that God Himself buried him after his death. (Num.20:12; Deut.34:6)

v. Moses, an extra-ordinary leader, with whom God spoke face to face...
Since Moses was prepared by God to die to self, God honored him as His chosen servant and revealed to him **every event that happened in the past, from the beginning of creation,** mentioned in the Book of Genesis, for example, how God Almighty created the heavens and the earth, how He formed man out of dust, how the first man Adam fell into sin, the redemption plan of God, etc.

It is amazing that God revealed to Moses not only the family line of Seth, the righteous son of Adam but also the family of Cain, the wicked son of Adam, who murdered his brother Abel. God also disclosed to Moses in detail the genealogy of Noah and the descendants of Noah's three sons, Shem, Ham and Japheth, after the flood destroyed the earth.

Can you imagine God would make known to Moses **every small event that had happened in the lives of our forefathers, Abraham, Isaac, Jacob and Joseph?** Prophets of God have foretold only the future events but God revealed to Moses whatever had happened in the past, the events that took place even before his birth. How awesome it is that God would speak to Moses like this face to face!

II. *Joseph, Purified by God's Word in the Prison*

Joseph was another chosen vessel whom God prepared for 13 years before he was appointed second to Pharaoh of Egypt.

1. God's Way—Troubled Path But Victorious End!

i. Joseph, Enrolled in God's School of Training... God revealed to Joseph his calling through dreams when he was very young. (Gen.37:5-11)

The Lord allowed him to be separated from his father Jacob, though he was his favorite son. God permitted Joseph to be thrown *into the pit* by his jealous brothers and then to be *sold as a slave* to work in Potiphar's house in Egypt. God's mighty hand was behind it all but God stopped Joseph's brothers from killing him. (Gen.37:12-36; 39:1-6)

ii. Reverential Fear of God protected Joseph from Adultery... While Joseph was a slave in Potiphar's house, he was *tempted by Potiphar's wife* to commit adultery. Though Joseph ran away from the sin because of the great fear of God that was in him, *yet God allowed him to be put in the prison.* But God protected Joseph from being killed. (Gen.39:7-23)

God's favor was upon Joseph every step of the way. Even in the prison he found favor in the eyes of the jailer. (Gen.39:20-23)

Though Joseph was righteous and ran away from the sin of adultery, yet *God did not rescue him from disgrace.* He had to endure the shame of being called an adulterer.

iii. Acting in the Flesh before God's Timing is Useless... In the prison Joseph accurately interpreted the dreams of the Pharaoh's cupbearer and baker. When the cupbearer was released as prophesied by Joseph, he requested the cupbearer to put in a good word to the Pharaoh about him. The Lord caused the cupbearer to forget about Joseph until it was God's timing to get Joseph out of prison, i.e., after 2 years. Joseph acted in the flesh but it did not work out for him *because the vessel was not fully prepared yet.* (Gen.40-41)

iv. The Word of God Prepared Joseph in the Prison... While Joseph was in the prison, they hurt his feet with fetters and he was laid in irons. Until the time that God's promises came to pass, the Word of the Lord tested Joseph, purified him and molded his character. (Ps.105:18-19)

v. Intimacy with God through Prayer... Joseph must have developed a very close relationship with God during those two years he spent in prison that when Pharaoh sent for him, Joseph was ready to interpret his dreams. God had filled Joseph with so much of wisdom, knowledge and the gifts of the Holy Spirit that he not only interpreted the dreams but he also gave solutions to the problem and rescued the whole nation of Egypt from famine. (Ps.105:16-22)

vi. God honored Joseph's good attitude...Joseph had all the reasons to murmur yet he ***never murmured against God*** even when he was in the prison. In due time, God lifted him up and made him second to the Pharaoh of Egypt. (Gen.41:39-43)

In another instance, when Joseph had an opportunity to take revenge on his brothers who were the cause for all his problems, yet ***he chose to forgive*** them and also met all their needs during the times of famine. (Gen.45)

2. Our Way Based on God's Way

i. Every day we must wait on the Lord to be filled with the Presence and the Power of the Holy Spirit so that we can crucify our fleshly desires on the cross and 'Die to Self.' Then God will be able to use us mightily.

ii. When you are half way through with God's training, you may feel like you are ready and you want to escape from the trials and the rest of the training, like how Joseph acted in the flesh and anticipated his release from the prison with the help of Pharaoh's cupbearer, before God's timing. But God will keep you in the same situation until you overcome your flesh and 'Die to Self.' He will put you through the furnace of fire until your faith is purified as gold.

III. *God Chased After Jonah, for He was a Prepared Vessel*

i.God will not let go off a Prepared Vessel... Jonah was a prepared vessel of God. This is the reason why God chased him around and would not let go off Jonah when he ran away from God's calling. ***God even used a***

great storm, a raging sea and a whale to make him repent and be obedient to His will; *for a prepared vessel cannot turn back on God's calling*. (Jonah 1-2; Lk.9:62)

ii. God taught the disappointed Jonah, His Ways... After being in the whale's belly for three days and three nights, finally, Jonah obeyed God and prophesied the destruction of Nineveh.

When the people of Nineveh truly repented, *God chose not to destroy the city of Nineveh*. This angered Jonah. He showed a bad attitude because it affected his reputation as a prophet.

God had to teach Jonah His ways and make him understand *God's heart for lost souls* through an analogy of a tree. (Jonah 2-4)

iii. *Jonah knew his God...*When God did not destroy Nineveh and did not bring Jonah's prophesy to pass, it displeased Jonah exceedingly and he was very angry and he said to God, "I know that You are a *gracious and merciful God, slow to anger and abundant in loving kindness, One who relents from doing harm*." (Jonah 4:1-2)

Do you know Your God like Jonah did? When you are in God's School of Training, God will be patient with you and work with your personality until He makes you into His image. He will teach you His ways.

IV. *Jesus gave up on the Pharisees, Though Teachers of God's Law, For They Resisted the Spirit of God*

i. Pharisees, Wise in their Own Eyes, missed Jesus, their Messiah... The Pharisees, the teachers of the Law, did not recognize their Messiah, Jesus Christ, who was in their midst.

ii. Pharisees Crucified Jesus, their Messiah on the Cross... The Pharisees were so *proud* of their knowledge of the Law that they refused to accept Jesus as the Son of God, though Jesus repeatedly tried to convince them of His deity. They were the ones who eventually put Him to death on the cross. (Jn.11:45-53)

iii. Pharisees Relied On Their Own Wisdom.... The Pharisees reasoned in their minds and *assumed that Jesus had come from the city of Nazareth* in Galilee while the Old Testament Scriptures clearly indicated that the Messiah would come from Bethlehem of Judah. *The Pharisees did not check out where Jesus was born nor did they enquire with His mother, Mary or His siblings.* (Mic.5:2; Jn.7:41-42, 52; Mk.6:1-3)

iv. Jesus allowed the Pharisees to Perish in their Blindness... Jesus was born in the city of Bethlehem but *He did not reveal it to the Pharisees* because their attitude towards Him was not right. At one point Jesus even said to the Pharisees, "You are of your father the devil." (Mic.5:2; Jn.8:12-47)

v. God had to let go off the Pharisees, the Teachers of God's Word, who were unyielding to His Spirit... On one occasion, when Jesus had cast out the demons by the Spirit of God, the Pharisees said that He cast out demons by Beelzebub, the prince of demons, thereby *committing the unpardonable sin of blasphemy against the Holy Spirit.* (Matt.12:24-32; Lk.11:15)

vi. Eternal Damnation for willfully Rejecting the Messiah... On several occasions, Jesus tried to convince the Pharisees that He is the Son of God, He is the way to Heaven and He is the Bread of Life that came down from Heaven but they willfully rejected Him as their Savior and did not understand God's ways. Therefore, God allowed the Pharisees, the teachers of God's law, to die in their sin and go to hell. Jesus even rebuked the Pharisees by calling them, *"Serpents, brood of vipers! How can you escape the condemnation of hell?"* (Matt.23)

vii. *God let go off the Unyielding Pharisees but not Jonah, the Prepared Vessel...* Though the Pharisees were the teachers of God's Word, God still had to let go off them because they were not yielding to His Spirit to *Die to Self."*

viii. *Be Warned...* Like the Pharisees, if we ignore the convictions of the Holy Spirit and harden our hearts to such an extent, then it is sad that God will be forced to give up on us too.

ix. *Today, if you will hear His voice, do not harden your Hearts as in the rebellion...* Scripture says, "Beware, brethren, lest there be in any of you *an evil heart of unbelief in departing from the living God*; but exhort one another daily, while it is called "Today," lest any of you be *hardened through the deceitfulness of sin."* (Heb.3:7-8, 12-13)

V. *King David, Transformed Into A Man of Prayer During God's Training Process*

i. David, Chosen to be a King, prepared by God for 13 years... At the age of 17, God anointed David, a little shepherd boy, to be the next king of Israel but first God had to take him through the process of preparation. (1 Sam.16:1-13)

*ii. David's Total Dependence on God...*For the next 13 years, as a part of God's training, David had to flee from King Saul who was after his life. It was difficult for David to hide in that small country of Israel and in the surrounding neighborhood. Many times he was just a foot away from death. During those perilous times David held on to God and *God was his only refuge.* (1 Sam.19-23)

David said, "The Lord is my rock and *my fortress* and *my deliverer; my God, my strength* in whom I will trust; my buckler and the horn of my salvation and my high tower. (Ps.18)

*iii. David's Amazing Love for God...*During his flight from King Saul, David sang numerous *heart touching psalms* as no one else had ever sung before, expressing his love for God. (Ps.18)

*iv. David, A Man of Prayer...*David talked to God all the time from the depth of his heart through his psalms. *David knew his God.* (Ps. 3-7; 10; 13; 17; 20; 22; 25; 32; 51; 54; 60; 61)

David developed an intimate relationship with God during those 13 years of training before he became the king of Israel at age 30. *David fulfilled the will of God for his life in his generation*. (Ps. 40:8; Acts 13:36)

*v. David's passion for God's Word...*We learn how to pray and talk to God through David's heartfelt psalms. He longed for God's Word with such passion that he repeatedly brings out in his psalms, the significance of God's Commandments, Statutes, Testimonies and the Law of the Lord. (Ps.19:7-14; 40:8)

VI. *God's Chosen Vessel in the Furnace of Fire*

*i. God is the Potter & We are the Clay...*The potter takes the clay and molds it into a beautiful clay pot but the process is not over yet. If the vessel is just sun-dried, it will break easily. So the potter has to put the vessel in the furnace of fire (900 degrees F). He then cools it and repeats this process over and over again several times till the clay pot becomes hardened to sustain the pressure. This process turns the ordinary clay into an exquisite piece of vessel ready for use, even in a royal palace. (Jer.18:1-12)

*ii. Vessel taken through the Cave of Afflictions...*God takes us through the cave of afflictions, the furnace of fire, *to remove all the dross of 'self, ego & I'* from us until we are refined as pure gold ready for the Master's use, just like how the potter molds the clay.

God knows that without the extreme heat of the fiery trials we will not be strong enough *to resist the crushing blows of Satan*.

God will not settle for 80% of yielding but will wait till the vessel is 100% ready for His use. We have to keep pressing on to fulfill 100% of God's will for our lives. (Is.64:8)

PART IV

Commandments Of God From
The Book Of Colossians

Book Of Colossians

Apostle Paul, while in prison for Christ, addressed this epistle to the *faithful believers* in Colosse in the year A.D.62. It is at times considered as a *"twin letter" with Ephesians,* because both epistles are similar in content and were written in the same year.

The Colossian church in Asia Minor may have been founded as a result of Paul's extraordinary three year ministry at Ephesus. (Acts 20:31)

The main theme of this letter is the "Deity and Supremacy of Christ."

Special features… This letter strongly affirms *Christ's Divinity*, to oppose the dangerous false teachings in Colosse.

It emphasizes…

1. The truth of *Christ's Supremacy* in creation and redemption. (Col.1:13-23)

2. That *Christ is the Son of God.* (Col.2:9)

3. That Jesus is the *image of the invisible God.* (Col.1:15)

4. That Jesus is the *fullness of the God head* in bodily form. (Col. 2:9)

5. That Jesus is the *Creator of all things.* (Col. 1:16-17)

6. That Jesus is the *Head of the Church.* (Col. 1:18)

7. That Christ is the *all-sufficient One* for our salvation. (Col. 1:14)

Apostle Paul says, *"Put it into practice*—whatever you have learned, or received or heard from me, or seen in me." (Phil. 4:9/NIV)

1. Be Rooted & Built Up In Christ

COMMANDMENTS OF GOD FOR US TO OBEY	REWARDS FOR OBEDIENCE/ SUPPORTING SCRIPTURES
As you have received Christ Jesus, the Lord... i. so walk in Him, ii. rooted and built up in Him, iii. established in the *faith,* iv. and abounding in the *Word* with *thanksgiving.* (Col.2:6-7)	i. So that you will be disciplined and *your faith in Christ will be firm.* - Apostle Paul (Col.2:5/NIV) ii. Lest anyone should *deceive you with persuasive words.*—Apostle Paul. (Col.2:4)

❖ *To have Revival in your Spirit, you should plead with the Lord, to fill you with the following:*

- Spirit of Reverential Fear of God. (Is.11:2)

- Spirit of Humility. (Is.57:15)

- Spirit of Conviction & Repentance of sins. (Ps.51:17)

- Spirit of Obedience to keep God's Commandments. (Matt.5:19; Jn.14:15)

- Spirit of Surrender & Dependence on God. (Gal.2:20; Rom.8:26)

- Spirit of Prayer & Intercession. (2 Chr.7:14; Ezek.22:30)

- Spirit of the Lord - 7 fold Spirit. (Is.11:2)

The Holy Bible –
The Most Read Book in the World

1.1. Jesus' Name Is "The Word of God"

Some interesting facts about the Bible, the Word of God...

- *Past, Present & Future of Mankind Revealed...*The Holy Bible is the only book which states the origin of the world, creation of man, his journey on earth and also the events that will happen in future. (Gen.1-3; Rev.1-22)

- *The Universal Book...*The Holy Bible is universal and known around the world and there has never been a book written like it ever before.

- *A Historical Book...*The Holy Bible is written from actual human history. You can absolutely rely on it.

- *The Most Translated Book...*The Holy Bible is the only book in the world that has partially or totally been translated into more than about *1200 languages* and dialects. How amazing!

- *The First Printed Book...*The Holy Bible was printed in 1454 and it holds the honor of the first book to be printed.

- *The Holy Spirit Inspired Book...*The Holy Bible is written from 3 different continents—*Asia, Africa and Europe*, by *40 authors* inspired by the Holy Spirit of God. (2 Tim.3:16-17)

- *The Most Sold Book...*The Holy Bible is the most sold book than any other book in the world; about *50 copies are being sold every minute*.

- *The Most Shoplifted Book...*The Holy Bible is the most shoplifted book in the world.

- *The Most Read Book...*It is reported that the Holy Bible is the most read book among all the books in the world.

- *The Holy Book that offers protection to your children...* The Lord says that if you forget My Word, I will forget your children. (Hosea 4:6)

- *The Only Life Changing & Life Giving Book...* God's Word is infallible, sacred, holy and true. It has been proven time and time again that millions of lives have been changed by the precious Word of God.

- *Don't you want to read this most popular Book called The Holy Bible?*

Jesus is the Word of God!

(Rev.19:13)

2. Be Not Deceived By The Tradition Of Men

COMMANDMENTS OF GOD FOR US TO OBEY	REWARDS FOR OBEDIENCE/ SUPPORTING SCRIPTURES
Beware lest anyone *cheat you through philosophy* and empty deceit...	i. For in Christ dwells *all the fullness of the Godhead* bodily. (Col.2:9)
i. according to the tradition of men,	ii. *You are complete in Christ.* (Col.2:10)
ii. according to the basic principles of the world,	iii. Christ is the *head of all principality* and power. (Col.2:10)
iii. and not according to Christ. (Col.2:8)	

3. Be Renewed In The Image Of Your Creator

Commandments concerning the following two topics covered in this Chapter will help you to be renewed in the image of your Creator:

- Put off the Old Man
- Put on the New Man

*Put off your old self...*If you live as you like, according to the worldly standard of righteousness, it will lead to *your spiritual death and eventually eternal damnation*; for Jesus says, *"Wide is the gate and broad is the road that leads to destruction, and many enter through it."* Hence you need to daily deny yourself of sinful pleasures of this world by the power of the Holy Spirit. (Matt.7:13/NIV; Lk.9:23)

A true Christian cannot be comfortable in habitual sin because the Holy Spirit will convict him as soon as he commits sin. (Jn.16:8)

*Put on your new self...*Jesus says, "Narrow is the gate and difficult is the way which leads to life, and there are few who find it." After you are born again, as a new believer in Christ, you should *walk in the narrow path of your Savior by obeying the commandments of God; for God's commandment is Eternal Life*. (Matt.7:14; Jn.12:50)

If you were raised with Christ, then *seek those things which are above*, where Christ is, seated at the right hand of God. When Christ who is our life appears, *you also will appear with Him in* glory. (Rom.6:4-11; 8:19; Col.3:1)

Set your mind on things above, not on things on the earth. For you died and now your life is hidden in Christ. Therefore, you must imitate Jesus by putting on the new man, manifesting all the 9 *"Fruit of the Holy Spirit."* (Rom.6:4-11; Gal.5:22-24)

As a believer in Christ, *whatever you do in word or deed, do all in the name of the Lord Jesus*, giving thanks to God the Father through Him. (Col.3:17)

3.1. Put Off The Old Man

COMMANDMENTS OF GOD FOR US TO OBEY	REWARDS FOR OBEDIENCE/ SUPPORTING SCRIPTURES
Die to Self: 1. Put to death, whatever belongs to your earthly nature: *Sexual immorality,* Impurity, Lust, Evil desires and *Greed*, which is idolatry. (Col.3:5/NIV)	Because of these things the *wrath of God is coming upon the sons of disobedience,* in which you also once walked when you lived in them. (Col.3:6-7)
Get Rid of the Sinful Nature: 2. You must rid yourselves of all such things as these... *Anger,* Rage, Malice, Slander and *Filthy language* from your lips. (Col.3:8/NIV) 3. Do not lie to each other. (Col.3:9/NIV)	i. Since you have taken off your old self with its practices. (Col.3:9/NIV) ii. You have *put on the new self,* which is being renewed, in knowledge in the *image of its Creator.* (Col.3:10/NIV)

3.2. Put On The New Man

COMMANDMENTS OF GOD FOR US TO OBEY	REWARDS FOR OBEDIENCE/ CONSEQUENCES OF DISOBEDIENCE/ SUPPORTING SCRIPTURES
Fruit of the Holy Spirit: 1. Clothe yourselves with… Compassion, Kindness, Humility, Gentleness and Patience. (Col.3:12/NIV)	For you are God's chosen people, holy and dearly loved. (Col.3:12/NIV)
Forgiveness: 2. *Bear* with each other and *forgive* whatever grievances you may have against one another. (Col.3:13/NIV) 3. Forgive as the Lord forgave you. (Col.3:13/NIV)	i. Even as Christ forgave you, so you also must do. (Col.3:13) ii. For if you do not forgive others their sins, your Father will not forgive your sins. (Matt.6:15/NIV)
Love: 4. Over all the above virtues, **put on love.** (Col.3:14/NIV)	For love binds them all together in perfect unity. (Col.3:14/NIV)
Peace of Christ: 5. Let the peace of Christ rule in your hearts and be thankful. (Col.3:15/NIV)	Since as members of one body you were called to peace. (Col.3:15/NIV)

COMMANDMENTS OF GOD FOR US TO OBEY	REWARDS FOR OBEDIENCE/ CONSEQUENCES OF DISOBEDIENCE/ SUPPORTING SCRIPTURES
The Word of Christ: 6. *Let the Word of Christ dwell in you richly...* i. As you teach and admonish one another with all wisdom. ii. As you sing psalms, hymns and spiritual songs with gratitude in your hearts to God. (Col.3:16/NIV)	For you have put on the new self, which is *being renewed, in knowledge* in the image of its Creator. (Col.3:10/NIV)
Your Words & Deeds: 7. *Whatever you do...* i. whether in word or deed, ii. do it all in the Name of the Lord Jesus, iii. giving thanks to God the Father through Him. (Col. 3:17/NIV)	*For you are God's chosen people, holy* and dearly loved. (Col.3:12/NIV)

- **Tremble at God's Word**...The Lord God Almighty states, "These are the ones I look on with favor: those who are humble and contrite in spirit, and who tremble at My Word." (Is.66:2/NIV)

- **God's Word accomplishes His Purpose**...The Sovereign Lord declares, "So is My Word that goes out from My mouth: *It will not return to Me empty*, but will accomplish what I desire and achieve the purpose for which I sent it." (Is.55:10-11/NIV)

4. Christ Is All And In All

COMMANDMENT OF GOD FOR US TO OBEY	REWARDS FOR OBEDIENCE/ SUPPORTING SCRIPTURES
Put on the new self, which is being renewed in knowledge in the image of its Creator. (Col.3:10/NIV)	*When you are renewed in the image of Christ*, then there is neither... i. Greek nor Jew, ii. circumcised nor uncircumcised, iii. barbarian, Scythian, slave nor free, iv. but **Christ is all and in all.** (Col.3:11)

Points to Ponder...

- *Everyone is precious in God's eyes...*When you put on the new self, you are being renewed in the image of your Creator, Jesus Christ. Then you will see people as Christ sees them, for every human being is created in His image and Jesus Christ has bought every person with His most precious blood.

- *Abide in Christ...*Jesus says that if we abide in Him, He will abide in us. When Christ dwells in you, you are transformed into His image. (Jn.15:5)

5. Do Not Let Anyone Disqualify You For The Prize

COMMANDMENTS OF GOD FOR US TO OBEY	CONSEQUENCES OF DISOBEDIENCE/ SUPPORTING SCRIPTURES
1. Do not let anyone who delights in false humility and the *worship of angels* disqualify you for the prize. (Col.2:18/NIV)	i. For such a person who worships angels goes into great detail about what he has seen, and his *unspiritual mind puffs him up with idle notions.* (Col.2:18/NIV) ii. For he has *lost connection with the Head,* (Christ) from whom the whole body, supported and held together by its ligaments and sinews, grows as God causes it to grow. (Col.2:19/NIV)
2. Do not subject yourself to the regulations (ways) of the world. (Col. 2:20/NIV)	i. For you have *died with Christ* to the *elemental spiritual forces* (fallen angels) of this world. ii. If you submit to the rules of the world, it is as though *you still belong to the world.* (Col.2:20/NIV)
3. Do not submit to the rules of the world... *"Do not handle! Do not taste! Do not touch!"* which are based on merely *human commands and teachings.* (Col. 2:21-22/NIV)	1. For these rules, which have to do with things that are *all destined to perish with use,* are based on merely human commands. (Col. 2:22/NIV) 2. For such regulations indeed... i. have an *appearance of wisdom,* ii. with their *self-imposed worship,* iii. their false humility and iv. their *harsh treatment of the body,* v. but *they lack any value in restraining sensual indulgence.* (Col. 2:23/NIV)

5.1. Satan Appears As Angel of Light

- *Worship of fallen angels...*The fallen angels that fell along with Satan when he rebelled against God, **can appear to human beings as gods.** Do not be deceived by these supernatural encounters of fallen angels. (1 Pet.3:19; Rev.12:9)

- Even Christians can be deceived *if they lose connection with the Head, Jesus* Christ.

- *Self Imposed Worship...* Apostle Paul also talks about rules concerning heathen worship, which appear wise and godly but they are merely teachings of men.

- *Rituals cannot buy forgiveness of sins...*The heathen religious leaders make people believe that they can please God by the harsh treatment of their bodies and they convince people that by following such rituals their sins will be forgiven.

- *No power to overcome sin...* The heathens practice only a "self-imposed religion" which does not give them any power to overcome the sins of the flesh. How sad!

6. God Reconciles You To Himself Through Christ

COMMANDMENTS OF GOD FOR US TO OBEY	REWARDS FOR OBEDIENCE/ SUPPORTING SCRIPTURES
1. Continue in the faith, grounded and steadfast. (Col.1:23) 2. Do not move away from the hope of the gospel.—Apostle Paul. (Col.1:23)	i. *Salvation*...You, who once were *alienated* and *enemies in your mind* by wicked works, *Christ has reconciled to God,* in the body of His flesh through death. (Col.1:21-22) ii. *Perfection*...If you continue in the steadfast faith in Christ, then He will *present you holy, and blameless, and above reproach* in God's sight - Apostle Paul. (Col.1:22-23)

- Salvation is the free gift of God (to your spirit) but to be perfect in the eyes of God, you have to work out your own salvation with fear and trembling, by obeying His Commandments. (Phil.2:12-13)

How To Be Born Again?

Steps to follow - as simple as **A, B, C**...

- **Admit** that you are a sinner before God, and truly repent of all your sins. (Rom.3:23)

  Ask God to forgive you; for He is faithful and just to forgive. (Prov.28:13)

  Accept God's forgiveness by faith; for it is a *free gift*. (Eph.2:8; 1 Pet.1:9)

- **Believe** in your heart that Christ died for your sins and rose up from the dead. (Rom.10:9)

- **Confess** with your mouth Jesus Christ as your Savior and Lord; and then you shall be *saved* and be *born again*. (Rom.10:9)

  Pray...Invite Jesus into your heart right now and ask Him to cleanse your heart with His precious blood and fill you with *peace* that the world cannot give you. (Rev.3:20; Jn.14:27)

  Reward...You will be rewarded with *"Eternal Life"* for being born again. (Jn.3:3,16)

7. Holiness In Family Life

COMMANDMENTS OF GOD FOR US TO OBEY	CONSEQUENCES OF DISOBEDIENCE/ SUPPORTING SCRIPTURES
Submission: 1. Wives, submit to your own husbands. (Col.3:18) 2. Husbands, love your wives and do not be harsh with them. (Col.3:19/NIV)	As is fitting in the Lord. (Col.3:18)
3. Children, obey your parents in everything. (Col.3:20)	For *this is well pleasing to the Lord.* (Col.3:20)
4. Fathers, *do not provoke* your children. (Col.3:21)	Lest they become *discouraged.* (Col.3:21)
Prayer: 5. Devote yourselves to prayer, being watchful and thankful. (Col.4:2/NIV)	Watch and pray that ye enter not into temptation. (Matt. 26:41)

Watch & Pray:

- In order to maintain holiness in family life – love, unity and peace between husband and wife and parents and children, *continual prayer and obedience* to the Lordship of Christ is required.

- If you are not watchful in prayer, Satan, our enemy, will find a way to enter inside of your family and create havoc in your life.

- Ask the Lord to put the *wall of fire* around your family.

8. Holiness In Work Life

COMMANDMENTS OF GOD FOR US TO OBEY	REWARDS FOR OBEDIENCE/ CONSEQUENCES OF DISOBEDIENCE/ SUPPORTING SCRIPTURES
Employees... 1. Servants, obey your earthly masters in everything. (Col.3:22/NIV) 2. Do it, *not only when their eye is on you* and to win their favor, but with sincerity of heart and reverence for the Lord. (Col.3:22/NIV)	i. Whatever you do, work at it *with all your heart,* as working for the Lord, not for human masters, since you know that you will *receive an inheritance from the Lord as a reward.* (Col.3:23-24/NIV) ii. It is the Lord *Christ you are serving.* (Col.3:24/NIV) iii. Anyone who does *wrong will be repaid* for his wrong, and there is no favoritism with God. (Col.3:25/NIV)
Employers... 3. Masters, provide your servants with what is *right and fair.* (Col.4:1/NIV)	Because you know that you also have a Master in Heaven. (Col.4:1/NIV)

9. Know The Mystery Of God, Christ Jesus

COMMANDMENTS OF GOD FOR US TO OBEY	REWARDS FOR OBEDIENCE/ CONSEQUENCES OF DISOBEDIENCE
Be encouraged in heart and united in love so that… i. You may have the *full riches of complete understanding*. ii. You may *know the mystery of God, namely, Christ*. iii. You may know Christ in whom are *hidden all the treasures of wisdom* and knowledge.—Apostle Paul. (Col.2:2-3/NIV)	i. Lest anyone should *deceive you* with persuasive words. - Apostle Paul. (Col.2:4) ii. For *God willed to make known* to His people among the gentiles, what are the riches of the *glory of this mystery, which is Christ in you*, the hope of glory. (Col.1:27)

I Am Jesus' And Jesus Is Mine!

This Must Be Your Heart's Cry -

o   I want to love Jesus more, in depth. (Matt.22:37; Jn.14:21; Phil.1:9)
o   I want to know Jesus better, as my Bridegroom. (Hos.2:19-20)
o   *I want to please my Jesus,* at any cost. (1 Thess.4:1-5)
o   I want to live for Jesus as apostle Paul. (Phi.1:21)
o   I want to walk with Jesus, as Enoch walked with God. (Gen.5:24)
o   I want to spend time with Jesus, my Best Friend. (Jn.15:14-15)
o   *I want to be one with Jesus,* in unity. (Jn.17:21)
o   I want to enjoy Jesus, who is sweeter than honey. (Ps.19:10; 119:103)
o   I want to have Jesus, in His fullness. (Eph.4:13; Col.1:19; 2:9)
o   I want to dwell with Jesus, my Beloved. (Jn.14:21, 23)
o   *I want to see Jesus,* as a Priest before God. (Acts 22:14; Rev.1:5)
o   I want to hear Jesus in much more clarity. (Acts 22:14; Jn.10:27)
o   I want to know Jesus' will for my life. (Matt.7:21)
o   I want to be in Christ, my righteousness. (1 Cor.1:30)
o   I want to live and move and have my being in Christ. (Acts 17:28)
o   I want to sup with Jesus at His banqueting table. (Rev.3:20)
o   I want to be in the mystery of God's will. (Eph.1:9)
o   *I want to be His bride* at the wedding feast of the Lamb, Jesus. (Rev.19:7)

Supremacy Of Jesus Christ, The Son Of God

1. The Son of God, Jesus *Christ is the image of the invisible God*.

2. Jesus is the firstborn (*preeminent*) over all creation.

3. By Jesus Christ *all things were created:*

   i. things in heaven and on earth,

   ii. visible and invisible,

   iii. whether thrones or dominions or principalities or powers.

4. All things were *created through Jesus and for Jesus.*

5. Jesus Christ is before all things.

6. *In Christ, all things consist.*

7. *Jesus is the head* of the body, the church;

   Jesus is *the beginning;*

   Jesus is *the firstborn* from the dead;

   that in all things Jesus may have the preeminence.

8. For it pleased the Father that *in Christ all the fullness* should dwell.

9. By Christ, God *reconciled all things* to Himself.

10. By Jesus, God reconciled all things to Himself, whether things on earth or things in heaven, He made peace through Jesus' blood shed on the cross. (Col.1:15-20)

"I Died on the Cross for You,
What Have You Done for Me?"

10. Make the Most of Every Opportunity To Win The Lost Souls

COMMANDMENTS OF GOD FOR US TO OBEY	REWARDS FOR OBEDIENCE/ CONSEQUENCES OF DISOBEDIENCE
Believers... 1. *Pray for us,* Servants of God - Apostle Paul. (Col.4:3/NIV)	i. So that God may *open a door* for the message of Christ. (Col.4:3/NIV) ii. That the Servants of God may *proclaim the mystery of Christ.* (Col.4:3/NIV) iii. That they may proclaim it *clearly,* as they should.—Apostle Paul. (Col.4:4/NIV) iv. In order that whenever the servants of God speak, *words may be given* to them so that they will *fearlessly make known the mystery of the Gospel*, as they should—Apostle Paul. (Eph.6:18-20/NIV)
2. Be wise in the way you act towards outsiders; *make the most of every opportunity.* (Col.4:5/NIV)	i. Preach the Word; be prepared in season and out of season. (2 Tim.4:2/NIV) ii. He who wins souls *is* wise. (Prov.11:30)
3. Let your *conversation* be always full of grace, seasoned with salt. (Col.4:6/NIV)	So that you may know *how to answer everyone.* (Col.4:6/NIV)
4. Take heed to the ministry which you have received in the Lord. (Col.4:17)	That you may fulfill it. (Col.4:17)

- *Preach the Gospel of Christ...*The gospel of Christ is bearing fruit and growing throughout the whole world. (Col.1:6/NIV)

- *Two Ways to get Eternal Rewards...*By living a lifestyle that reflects the *image of Christ* and by *winning souls* for God's Kingdom, you can receive rewards in Heaven. (Col.1:10; Prov.11:30; Dan.12:3)

10.1. Bear Fruits For The Gospel Of Christ

- *Hear the Gospel of Christ...*The Colossian church believers heard the truth of the gospel.

- *Comprehend the Grace of God...*They truly understood the grace of God that Jesus Christ died on the cross in their place.

- *Have Hope of Eternal Life...*They comprehended the hope that is laid up for them in heaven through the Word of God.

- *Possess Steadfast Faith in Christ...*This revelation increased their faith in Christ and their love for all the saints.

- *Bear Fruits for the Kingdom of God...*Then they started bearing fruits for the gospel of Christ. (Col.1:3-6)

- *Multiply Your Talents & Be Rewarded in Heaven...* As the Colossian church believers, when we truly understand what Jesus Christ has done for us on the cross and the hope that is stored up for us in heaven, we will also be motivated to bear fruits for the Kingdom of God and be rewarded accordingly in heaven. (Matt.25:21)

God Will Make You Accountable For the Lost Souls

The Lord says, "On your clothes is found the blood of the lives of the poor innocents, I have not found it by secret search, but plainly on all these things.

Yet you say, 'because I am innocent, surely His anger shall turn from me.' Behold, *I will plead My case against you, because you say, 'I am innocent.'"* (Jer.2:34-35)

Hence, do not live in luxury and in your comfort zone, lost in your own world, not caring about the things of God, when souls around you are perishing and going to hell, without knowing their Messiah, Jesus Christ.

Redeem your time. Time lost cannot be regained. *Time will delay no longer.* Be alert, watch and pray. *Jesus is coming back sooner than you expect!*

11. Present Every Man Perfect In Christ

COMMANDMENTS OF GOD FOR US TO OBEY	REWARDS FOR OBEDIENCE/ SUPPORTING SCRIPTURES
1. Preach Christ. 2. Warn every man and 3. Teach every man in all wisdom, as Apostle Paul did. (Col.1:28)	So that you may present every man perfect in Christ Jesus, as apostle Paul did. (Col.1:28)

Criteria for Perfection in Christ

When you have...

* 100% Reverential Fear of God. (Is.11:2)

* 100% Divine Love. (Rom.5:5; Matt.22:35-40; 1 Cor.13)

* 100% Obedience to God's Commandments - not 40%, 60% or 80%. (Jn.14:15-17; Matt.5:19; Is.59:1-2)

* 100% Surrender to God's will & God's ways. (Matt.16:24)

* 100% Dependence on God for everything. (Prov.3:5-6)

* 100% - Praying without ceasing. (1 Thess.5:17)

* 100% - Meditating on God's Word day and night. (Ps.1:2)

* 100% Victory over sin, Satan and the world. (1 Jn.2:15-17)

* 100% Dying to self, own wisdom & own ways. (Gal.2:20)

* 100% Transformed mind, with the Word of God. (Rom.12:2)

* 100% - Fullness of Christ. (Eph.4:11-13)

All this is possible when you are filled with the Holy Spirit without measure -100%; who is available to all and the only One who can make you perfect in Christ. (Jn.3:34; Joel 2:28; Jn.7:37-38; Rev.2,3)

12. Set Your Hearts & Minds On Things Above

COMMANDMENTS OF GOD FOR US TO OBEY	REWARDS FOR OBEDIENCE/ SUPPORTING SCRIPTURES
Since you have been *raised with Christ...* 1. Set your *hearts* on things above, where Christ is, seated at the right hand of God. (Col.3:1/NIV) 2. *Set your minds on things above,* not on earthly things. (Col.3:2/NIV)	i. *For you died* and your life is now hidden with Christ in God. (Col.3:3/NIV) ii. When *Christ, who is your life,* appears, then you also will *appear with Him in glory.* (Col.3:4/NIV)

Desire the following "Things of the Above" -

i.   *Spirit of Reverential Fear of God.* (Is.11:2)

ii. Spirit of Conviction & Repentance of sins. (Jn.14:15-17; Is.59:1-2; Lk.13:1-5)

iii. *Spirit of Obedience* to God's Commandments. (Matt.5:19; Matt.28:20; Ps.91)

iv. *Fire of the Holy Spirit* (Jn.3:13-18; Joel 2:28)

v.   7-Fold Holy Spirit. (Is.11:1-2)

vi. Spirit of Wisdom & Understanding. (Is.11:1-2)

vii. Spirit of Counsel & Might. (Is.11:1-2)

viii. Spirit of Knowledge & Revelation. (Is.11:1-2; Eph.1:16-17)

ix. Spirit of Humility. (Matt.5:5; Lk.18:14)

x.   *Ask for Visions & Dreams.* (Joel 2:28; Jer.33:3)

xi. Long to See Jesus & hear His voice, as His Sheep. (Matt.5:8; Acts 22:14; Jn.10:27)

xii. Know God's will for your life. (Acts 22:14; Matt.7:21)

xiii. Baptism of the Holy Spirit. (Matt.3:11; Acts 1:4-5; 1 Cor.12:13)

xiv. Latter rains & Former rains. (Joel 2:23, 28; Hos.6:3)

xv. *9 Fruits of the Holy Spirit* (Gal.5:22-23)

xvi. *9 Gifts of the Holy Spirit.* (1 Cor.12:4-11)

13. You Are Complete In Christ

COMMANDMENTS OF GOD FOR US TO OBEY	REWARDS FOR OBEDIENCE/ SUPPORTING SCRIPTURES
1. *Do not let anyone judge you...* i. by what you eat or drink, ii. or with regard to a religious festival, iii. or a New Moon celebration, iv. or a Sabbath day. (Col. 2:16/NIV) 2. Do not let anyone who delights in false humility and the *worship of angels disqualify you.* (Col.2:18/NIV)	1. These are a shadow of the things that were to come; *the reality, however, is found in Christ.* (Col.2:17/NIV) 2. *For You Are Complete In Christ...* *i. Circumcised by Christ...*In Christ, you are circumcised by putting off the sinful nature; not with the circumcision done by the hands of men but with the circumcision by Christ. (Col.2:10-11) *ii. Buried with Christ...*You are buried with Him in baptism. (Col.2:12) *iii. Raised with Christ...*You are raised with Him through your faith in the power of God, who raised Christ from the dead. (Col.2:12) *iv. Alive with Christ...*When you were dead in your sins and in the uncircumcision of your sinful nature, God made you alive with Christ. (Col.2:13)

COMMANDMENTS OF GOD FOR US TO OBEY	REWARDS FOR OBEDIENCE/ SUPPORTING SCRIPTURES

1. *Do not let anyone judge you...*
 	
  i. by what you eat or drink,
  ii. or with regard to a religious festival,
  iii. or a New Moon celebration,
  iv. or a Sabbath day. (Col. 2:16/NIV)
 	
These are a shadow of the things that were to come; *the reality, however, is found in Christ.* (Col.2:17/NIV)
 	
2. Do not let anyone who delights in false humility and the *worship of angels disqualify you.* (Col.2:18/NIV)
	For You Are Complete In Christ...
	
	*v. Forgiven by Christ...*Christ forgave us all our sins, having *cancelled the written code* with its regulations that was against us, and that stood opposed to us; He took it away, *nailing it to the Cross.* (Col.2:13-14/NIV)
	
	*vi. Christ Disarmed Principalities & Powers of Darkness...*Having disarmed the powers and authorities, Christ made a public spectacle of them. (Col.2:15/NIV)
	
	*vii. Christ Triumphed over the Powers of Darkness for you...*Christ, who is the head of all principality and power, has triumphed over the powers and authorities *by the Cross.* (Col.2:10,15)

*Jesus Christ is the True God and Eternal Life...*The reality is found in Christ and since *you are complete in the Lord Jesus Christ,* you don't need to worship any other deity or angels but Christ alone. (1 Jn.5:20)

"If You Love Me, Obey My Commandments"–Jesus

- *Eternal Life...God's Command is everlasting life.* – Jesus (Jn.12:50)

- *Right to the Tree of Life...*Blessed are those who *do Christ's Commandments* that they may have the right to the tree of life, and may *enter through the gates* into the city. (Rev.22:14)

- *See Jesus...*Jesus declared, "Whoever has *My commands* and keeps them is the one who loves Me and I too will love them and show Myself to them." (Jn.14:21)

- *Know Jesus...*By this we know that we know Him, if we keep His Commandments. He who says, "I know Him" and does *not keep His Commandments, is a liar,* and the truth is not in him. (1 Jn.2:3-5)

- *Blessings of God...*The Lord God Almighty says that if you diligently obey the voice of the Lord, your God, to *observe carefully all His Commandments,* all the blessings shall come upon you and overtake you. (Deut.28:1-14)

- *Save your Soul...*He who keeps the Commandment keeps his soul, but he who is careless of his ways will die. (Prov.19:16)

- *Be Rewarded...*Whoever *despises the Word* brings *destruction* on himself, but he who *reveres the Commandment* will be *rewarded.* (Prov.13:13)

- *Obey God's Commands...*In the last days, Satan, the dragon, will be enraged at the woman (Israel) and will wage war against the rest of her offspring - those who *keep God's commands* (OT) and hold fast their *testimony about Jesus* (NT). (Rev.12:17)

- *Keep Jesus' Commands...*This calls for patient endurance on the part of the people of God who keep His commands (OT) and remain faithful to Jesus (NT). (Rev.14:12; Jn.14:15-17)

- *Obedience to OT & NT Commands...*It is amazing to see that the last book of the Bible, the *Book of Revelation, emphasizes* that we should obey both the commandments of God (OT) and commandments of Christ (NT). (Rev.12:17; 14:12; 22:14)

"Go & Make Disciples of All the Nations,

Teaching them to Observe

All things that I have Commanded you" – Jesus

COMMANDMENTS OF GOD FOR US TO OBEY	REWARDS FOR OBEDIENCE/ CONSEQUENCES OF DISOBEDIENCE/
Duty of all Mankind: 1. Fear God and keep His Commandments. (Ecc.12:13)	i. For this is the duty of all mankind. ii. For God will bring every deed into judgment, including every hidden thing, whether it is good or evil. (Ecc.12:13-14/NIV)
Obedience to Jesus' Commandments: 2. Keep *My Commandments.* – Jesus (Jn.15:10)	i. For you will abide in My love. - Jesus (Jn.15:10) ii. That My joy may remain in you. - Jesus iii. And that *your joy may be full.* (Jn.15:11)
3. Do *whatever I command* you. - Jesus (Jn.15:14)	Then you are *My friends.* – Jesus (Jn.15:14-15)
4. Have *My Commandments* and keep them. – Jesus (Jn.14:21)	i. For it is he who loves Me. ii. He who loves Me will be loved by My Father. iii. I will love him. iv. And *I will manifest Myself to him.* - Jesus (Jn.14:21)
5. Keep My Word, if you love Me. - Jesus (Jn.14:23)	i. For My Father will love him. ii. **We will come to him.** iii. And make our home with him. - Jesus (Jn.14:23)

Preachers, Teach Everyone To Obey
All Of Jesus' Commandments

COMMANDMENTS OF GOD FOR US TO OBEY	REWARDS FOR OBEDIENCE/ CONSEQUENCES OF DISOBEDIENCE/
Teach Jesus' Commandments: 6. i. Go, ii. make disciples of all the nations, iii. baptizing them in the name of the Father and of the Son and of the Holy Spirit, iv. *teaching them to observe all things that I have commanded you.* - Jesus (Matt.28:19)	And lo, *I am with you always, even to the end of the age.* - Jesus (Matt.28:20)
Obedience to God's Commandments: 7. Do not break even the least of God's Commandments and teach men. - Jesus (Matt.5:19)	Or else, you will be called *least* in the Kingdom of Heaven. (Matt.5:19)
8. Obey God's Commandments and teach others so. – Jesus (Matt.5:19)	For you will be called *Great* in the Kingdom of Heaven. (Matt.5:19)

Obedience To God's Commandments Brings Blessings

COMMANDMENTS OF GOD FOR US TO OBEY	REWARDS FOR OBEDIENCE/ CONSEQUENCES OF DISOBEDIENCE/
Blessings for you & your children: 9. Observe and obey all these words which I command you. - Lord God Almighty (Deut.12:28)	That it may go well with you and your children after you forever, when you do what is good and right in the sight of the Lord your God. (Deut.12:28)
Prosperity & Good Success: 10. This Book of the Law shall not depart from your mouth, but you shall meditate in it day and night. 11. Observe to do according to all that is written in the Law. (Josh.1:8)	For then you will make your way prosperous, and then you will have good success. (Josh.1:8)
Righteousness in God's sight: 12. Hear and obey the Law. (Rom.2:13)	For it is not those who **hear the law** who are righteous in God's sight, but it is those who **obey the law** who will be declared righteous. (Rom.2:13/NIV)

Peace to the brothers and sisters,

Love with faith from God the Father
and the Lord Jesus Christ.

Grace to all who love our Lord Jesus Christ
with an undying love. (Eph.6:23-24)

"If you love Me, keep My Commandments." - Jesus
(Jn.14:15)

List of Articles in the Book

About The Author

TESTIMONY OF DR. ESTHER V. SHEKHER

Greetings in His Most Holy Name from Christ Rules Ministries!

Salvation Experience...I accepted Christ as my Lord and Savior at the age of 18. During the course of my salvation experience, two facts became crystal clear to me -

- *Jesus loved me so deeply that He would even die for me.*
- *Jesus hated sin so much that He would bear the suffering and shame of the cross to deliver me from that awful sin.*

I understood at that early age that I too must hate sin and I started longing for His righteousness. After yearning for the anointing of the Holy Spirit for a year, God filled me with His Spirit for about 3 hours.

Promise of God Fulfilled...Jesus Christ became my passion and I spent a lot of time talking to Him daily. Jesus became my best friend. While I was doing my medical training, one day, after crying out to the Lord for about 6 hours in desperation, longing to see Him, to hear His voice and to know His will for my life, the Lord promised me through the Scriptures *(Acts 22:14) that I would see the Just One, hear Him speak and know His will.* This promise came to pass 7 years later; for Jesus says, "My sheep will hear My voice."

Calling of God...The Lord brought me to America in 1989. I started spending 3-4 hours every day in fervent prayer and the Word. On March 18, 1992, while I was pouring my heart to God in prayer, I heard His *audible voice* saying, *"I died on the cross for you, what have you done for Me? Will you do my ministry until you have your last breath?"* From then on, I heard Him almost every night, waking me up at 3 a.m. saying, *"Stand in the gap and cry out in the middle of the night with agony for the perishing souls."* I have been obeying the Lord as He instructs me every single day. Our God is faithful in fulfilling His promises.

God molded my character over a period of several years by taking me through numerous trials and cave of afflictions. He trained me to die to self and to depend on Him instead of my own abilities. His awesome Presence, *His precious Holy Spirit, like a ball of fire cleanses the temple of my spirit everyday* and fills me, preparing me for His Ministry.

The Lord, in His grace, enrolled me in His School of Training. He prepared me by taking me through various trials, especially *the four major tests, namely, Character Test, Obedience Test, Word Test and Faith Test*, for the next 14 years. The tests got tougher and tougher and finally, to be honest before God, I felt like I was taking Ph.D. level exams in these four spiritual areas. Only by the grace of God, I could pass these tests according to God's standard of righteousness. All glory be to God!

Ministry Highlights:

*Mission Trip...*God called me as a full time Missionary and Evangelist in 2003. I obeyed His call and since then, I have been preaching the Gospel of Jesus Christ in many nations around the world, for the past 14 years.

*Pastors Conferences...*The Lord said to me, after preparing me for His calling for many years, *"Now you are worthy to preach to the Pastors and Believers of nations around the world."* The Lord Himself opened up opportunities for me to speak in Pastors' Conferences. I ended up speaking in about 40 Pastors' Conferences so far.

*Preaching Ministry...*I have also spoken in numerous Churches of various denominations, Bible Colleges, Prayer Revival Conferences, Women's Meetings, Youth Camps, Rural Outreach, etc., strengthening the believers and winning the lost to Christ. Praise be to God!

*"Christ Rules Ministries"...*The Lord enabled me to establish "Christ Rules Ministries" in 2008, to raise up fervent Intercessors and worthy Laborers for the Kingdom of God, to win the perishing souls to Christ.

International Prayer Network (IPN)...The Lord gave me a divine strategy to start prayer cells through International Prayer Network (IPN) which I established in 2010, to *intercede for the Salvation of every lost soul in America* and other nations of the world. I have successfully implemented this IPN Prayer Strategy in USA, Nicaragua, Sri Lanka, Malaysia, Singapore, India, Andaman Islands, etc. By God's grace, with the help of the Pastors and believers, more than *9000 Prayer Cells* have been started so far in these nations. Praise be to our God!

Prayer Ministry in USA... Since 2012, I have been preaching in several Churches in Stockton, Hayward, Galt and Bay Area in Northern California, Florida, Georgia, Washington DC and Maryland, etc. I have sowed the seed of prayer in the hearts of people, encouraging believers to intercede for the Salvation of every perishing soul living in these cities.

Publications...By God's grace, I have written 3 books so far, entitled, *"All the Commandments of God"* Volume I & II, and *"All the Commandments of Christ"*, which are published in USA. Jesus says, "If you love Me, obey My Commandments." The first book is a *checklist of Jesus' commandments* with their rewards and consequences clearly explained, from the Gospels of Matthew and John, covering all the major topics in Christian faith. This second book is also on the same concept of God's Commandments, taken from the Epistles of Apostle Paul. My third book entitled, *"All The Commandments of Christ"* is based on the same concept of Jesus' commandments with their rewards and consequences.

TV Ministry... By the grace of God, I started the TV Ministry in 2011 to preach on End Times, the Commandments of God, the God given strategy to start prayer cells in various nations and to prepare the churches to meet our Bridegroom, Jesus Christ in Rapture.

Presently, God has been opening TV interviews across America, based on my books. Praise be to our God!

Seminars on End Times...I have also been preaching on End Times and teaching the whole *"Book of Revelation"* using effective power-point presentations, to bring the awareness about the Second Coming of Jesus Christ, in various Churches.

Social work...Started Gypsy Literacy Programs, Widows Ministry, Handicapped Ministry, Orphanage Ministry, etc., in Asia and Nicaragua.

All the promises that the Lord has given me so far are coming to pass one by one. I humbly yield myself to the Master, to be used for His glory.

My desire is to fulfill His will each and every day of my life. Blessed be His Holy Name!

MINISTRY MOTTO: PRAY, GIVE, GO OR SEND FOR THE KINGDOM OF GOD

CHRIST RULES OFFICES

To Contact the Author, Write/Call:

In USA
Dr. Esther +1 (626) 450-5973
Michelle +1 (480) 251-1979
Darla +1 (209) 401-1696
Email: christrulesnations@gmail.com/christrulesus@hotmail.com
Website: www.christrulesnations.org /
allthecommandmentsofgod.com
Facebook: Christ Rules Nations

If this book has blessed you, please do write your
testimony and/or prayer requests.

In Singapore
Call Ms. Maya +65 81387856 / 65220096

In Malaysia
Contact: Pr. Nathaneal
E-07-12, PPR Muhibbah,
Jalan 15/55 of Jalan Puchong Taman,
Taman Muhibbah 58200, Kuala Lumpur, Malaysia.
Cell No. +60173204571

In India
Contact: Pr. Santhosh +91 9994709461 / 9789253631
Mr. Chinna +91 9171081108 / 9003232505

In Nicaragua
Contact: Pr. Francisco Castillo Andino + 505 3130418 / 6332290

Printed in the United States
By Bookmasters